MoMENTs
A Dad Holds On

By
Patrick L. Hempfing

Cherish the moments.
Patrick Hempfing

Foreword by J. Hempfing, Age 11

J. Hempfing

Praise for MoMENts

MoMENts: A Dad Holds On is not a parenting handbook, but one all parents should read. Patrick leaves the corporate world behind and discovers life as a stay-at-home dad is a job like no other. His tender, humorous stories contain little life lessons and serve as reminders to cherish the moments with family. ~ **Dahlynn McKowen,** *Not Your Mother's Book* **creator and** *Chicken Soup for the Soul* **co-author**

Patrick Hempfing delights as he lets readers in on the lessons and activities he shares with his daughter and how they affect him as a stay-at-home dad. *MoMENts: A Dad Holds On* includes quiet, tender moments and laugh-out-loud stories any parent will appreciate. Readers will enjoy seeing how he transforms daily chores into memorable adventures. ~ **Susan Weiss, Publisher of New York Parenting**

As the Editor of *Suburban Parent Magazines*, I would like to extend my thanks for Patrick Hempfing. As a writer for our publications for several years, he has entertained us and our readership with his humorous, witty, and inspiring columns of his life as a dad and husband. His MoMENts column is anticipated each month and always gets a great response. ~ **Mary Ellen Caldwell, Editor,** *Suburban Parent Magazines*

Thank you for creating such compelling work! ~ **Kirsten Flournoy, former Editor,** *San Diego Family Magazine*

Patrick Hempfing writes with honesty and wit about the moments that make the parenting journey worthwhile, delivering wisdom and hope to others on the same path. ~ **Jennifer Jhon, Editor,** *South Florida Parenting*

Patrick Hempfing's warm, inviting voice reaches out to readers, appealing to their own experiences as parents — with just the right dose of humor. ~ **Amanda Robison, former Editor,** *Metroparent*

Houston Family Magazine recently discovered Patrick Hempfing and quickly snatched him up as a regular columnist for our monthly magazine. His vignette portrayals of fatherhood are poignant, insightful, and funny, creating vivid images of moments that make parenting sweet, scary and, ultimately, the most rewarding job a person can undertake. Patrick's MoMENts columns are conversational and effortless, like the casual exchange of daily parental happenings you would enjoy at the park while the kids play on the swings. His work is simply delightful and a valued addition to our monthly content. ~ **Sara Stephens, Managing Editor,** *Houston Family Magazine* **and former Editor,** *Southeast Texas Family Magazine*

Patrick, a well-intentioned, loving – but not always perfect – father, beautifully writes with humor and humility about the trials and tribulations of modern-day parenting. He is a refreshing rarity in the publishing world representing the highs and lows of fatherhood, yet his message rings strong with all readers, no matter the gender. There is a little Patrick in us all. ~ **M. L. Ellen Percival, Publisher, *Calgary's Child Magazine***

Patrick Hempfing's columns share laugh-out-loud moments paired with striking insights. Funny and thought-provoking, a refreshing read. You can't help but smile and nod –MoMENts is always a favorite for our readers. ~ **Sharon Gowan, Publisher/Editor, *Sonoma Family Life Magazine* and *Mendo Lake Family Life Magazine***

Patrick Hempfing's touching reflections on fatherhood's roller coaster of emotions and experiences leave readers connecting with the sweet – and salty – moments he shares with his daughter. This is a must-read for any father who truly cherishes every fleeting second he shares with his child. ~ **Beth Shugg, Editor, *Carolina Parent***

Patrick Hempfing's positive parenting reflection in his MoMENts column is like a breath of fresh air, providing central PA readers with laughter and lessons. Writing from personal experience as a stay-at-home father, his column illuminates the intrinsic value of father involvement. Hempfing's perspective is written with clarity and humor. His MoMENts is undoubtedly destined to be shared with a broader audience – perhaps becoming the book that is taken to after-school sport practices, music lessons, tutoring, etc. ~ **Mari Conners, Editor,** *About Families*

Patrick Hempfing became a parent later in life, and I believe that has given his writing wonderful sensitivity, depth, and wisdom which easily reaches into both the minds and hearts of his readers. ~ **Michele Miller, Editor and Publisher,** *Western New York Family Magazine*

Patrick Hempfing has given *Palmetto Parent* a different perspective on parenting through a dad's eyes instead of just from moms'. His entertaining column about being a stay-at-home dad has been well received by our readers. We appreciate him greatly! ~ **Lori Coon, Publisher,** *Palmetto Parent*

Patrick Hempfing has a lot going for him as a highly creative writer and as an involved father. His MoMENts columns are warm without being maudlin and humorous without overreaching. He is a very positive part of our publication. ~ **Gaye Bunderson, Editor,** *Idaho Family Magazine*

Those of you who have kids, know kids, love kids, or simply WERE a kid will love anything written by Patrick Hempfing, a stay-at-home dad. Or, as I like to say, a "recovering accountant." ~ **Janet Sheppard Kelleher, columnist and author of** *Big C, little ta-ta,* **speaker, and internationally renowned ChemoHawk Mom**

Patrick Hempfing's MoMENts captures heartwarming stories sprinkled with humor that reflect a special bond between a father and a young daughter growing up. He's a writer not to be missed. ~ **Linda Joyce, author of the Fleur de Lis and Sunflower series**

Every time I read one of Patrick Hempfing's columns I think the same thing, "where was this guy when all my children were small?" I can't turn back the clock, but I do share the wisdom with my grown children as they rear their children. ~ **John House, MD, author of** *So Shall You Reap, Choices,* **and** *Trail of Deceit,* **2016 nominee, Georgia Author of the Year**

Patrick Hempfing shares the adventures of a stay-at-home dad – a dad who cherishes every moment as he and his daughter build memories. His column delights, charms, and warms my heart. His family exemplifies a modern and innovative family structure. Their successful endeavor is an encouraging example of family unity and strength. ~ **Mary Stripling, author of *Nonagenarian,* a collection of cherished moments with seasoned friends**

Patrick Hempfing is a creative writer who spins yarns about his daughter and his role as a Mr. Mom. Although writing about children may be old hat to some, Patrick's stories are always fresh and universal. He doesn't need exaggeration to provide the reader with a grin and sometimes a poignant tear or two, because Patrick's stories touch the heart as well as the funny bone. ~ **Cappy Hall Rearick, syndicated columnist and novelist, 2012 nominee, Georgia Author of the Year**

Table of Contents

Foreword..1

Acknowledgements 3

Introduction..5

Chapter 1: A Job Like No Other 9

Chapter 2: MoMENts of Learning......................15
   "Push the Button!" 16
   Happy Reading...19
   $3.84 22
   The Joy of Writing ... and Remembering.....................25
   The Wonders Ahead..28
   Learning to Chill...31
   Manatees Aren't Fat..34
   Pink Bunny...37
   The Gift of Laughter 41
   A Donkey, a Monkey, and a Cow....................44
   The Scent of a Kitchen 47

Chapter 3: MoMENts of Time Passing Quickly 51
   Dream Big...52
   Little in the Middle..55
   Staying Young...57

Operation Slow-Down...59
Summer Camp Fun 61
Holding On..64
Passes 67
I Will 70
Quite a Ride 73
The Right Number 76
Fields of Dreams..79

Chapter 4: MoMENts of Sighs and Surprise 83
Cherish the Moments...84
Call Me, Maybe..86
Embarrassing Love...88
Twists and Turns...91
Windows and Wheels...94
A Truckload of Kisses..97
I Hope You Twirl 100
When Life Throws You Branches.......................103
Sweeter than Icing..106
The Humbling Workout......................................109

Chapter 5: Holiday MoMENts.......................................113
I Love Me ... and My Family..............................114
Expressions of Love..117
Tails of Love...120
Leprechauns, Pots of Gold, and Clovers 123
A Wagon Filled with Memories.........................126
The Eggshausting Hunt 129

Take Time to Color 132

Labor of Love... 135

A Special Halloween 138

Half Full.. 141

The Quiet Thanksgiving 144

The Most Wonderful Time 147

The Best Gifts 150

Chapter 6: Father MoMENts 153

A Father's Pride.. 154

King... 158

Superdad.. 161

What Does the Dad Say? 164

I Grouchy: A Tired Dad's Story 167

A Dad's Wall of Joy 170

Chapter 7: Mother MoMENts............................ 173

I Want My Momma 174

I Still Need Mom.. 176

Lessons Learned.. 179

The Right Ingredients................................... 182

Thank You … at 70 words per minute 186

Spoken Words 189

Chapter 8: A Strong Finish 193

The Secret... 195

The Nine-Fingered Writer............................. 201

Hormone Collision 205

Being There...211

Jesus and Momma..217

Dog...Gone!...221

Wife or Dog...225

The List..228

Celebrate...232

Chapter 9: Conclusion 235

Epilogue 239

Foreword

As Daddy and I were driving home from my dance class, he posed a question to me. "Who do you think should write my foreword?" I thought about it for a minute, and then answered, "Me." We talked it over for a minute, and then I asked, "What is a foreword?" This is my first foreword ever.

My daddy is amazing! He always takes time to cherish the moments. He is very patient and very smart. The reason I wanted to write the foreword is because I have been here for all of the experiences! Even if I don't remember pretending to puke in the ice bucket, I do remember more recent stories. I think my daddy's book is a book about love, joy, and happiness. If you or someone you know is going through a hard time, you can always refer to this book! I recommend this book as a book of good things!

J. Hempfing, age 11

To my precious daughter:

I dedicate this book to you. Thank you for writing a touching foreword; three of your words jump out: love, joy, and happiness. You have filled your mom's and my life with more love, joy, and happiness than we could have ever imagined. When you read these stories as an

1

adult, I hope you'll remember all the wonderful experiences we had together. God blessed us with many happy moments to cherish.

Since love, joy, and happiness are good things, this is, for sure, a book of good things. May good things fill all of your days as you make your mark in this world, and may the beautiful sound of your laughter bless others as it has so richly blessed our family.

P. Hempfing, age 55

Acknowledgements

Most days, I feel I have the two best jobs in the world – stay-at-home dad and writer. At times, though, it seems they are two of the most challenging.

In some ways, writing this book was like having another child, except it took more than nine months of labor, and more than two people were involved in the creation. I owe thanks to all those who helped me deliver this book to market. Like many writers, I've benefitted from a strong support system, which is sort of like having Grandmommy on call when your infant won't stop crying.

Thank you to my wonderful wife, who spent hours polishing my stories while also working hard at her day job and being an excellent mother and role model to our daughter. I could not have accomplished my dream of being a published author without her.

Carole Silverman, who was my great boss in the Office of Inspector General at University of Florida, used to edit my audit reports. She now proofreads my stories and catches mistakes in my drafts. Like safety pins on old-style diapers, she makes sure no embarrassing material slips out.

I owe a big thank you to Debra and Meredith Brown from My Write Platform. I came to them with a manuscript and they delivered a published book. I felt the sting when they edited my writing, but they coached me through the pre-publishing issues and other labor pains – and our laughter functioned like an epidural when they cut out some of my words.

Thank you to John Alexander for his photography and cover layout and Danielle Pomeranz for capturing our concept in an innovative logo. Their work beautifully dressed my baby.

My writing friends from the Southeastern Writers Association have showered me with support. I am especially grateful to Cappy, Dahlynn, Jan, John, Ken, Lee, Linda, and Mary, who gifted me with their advice and encouragement.

My precious daughter provided the stories for this book, which are just a sample of the many wonderful moments we've cherished together. I let her read my drafts before they are published and she's been a tough evaluator. Like a doctor who points out the facts, she gives me reasons to work harder toward my goals.

Thank you, God, for all of these wonderful people and the others you've put in my path. You blessed me with a daughter, and the opportunity to love and nurture her as she grew from an infant into a beautiful 11-year-old young lady. This book expresses my appreciation for the privilege of being her dad.

Introduction

"Daddy, you can't pull me. That would be embarrassing!" My 9-year-old daughter, Jessie, uttered this statement during a recent stroll around our neighborhood. Our walk started out great as Jessie pulled her 22-pound Shetland sheepdog, Sadie, in her red Radio Flyer wagon. About halfway into the walk, Jessie became tired and sat down in the wagon to rest with Sadie. I grabbed the black wagon handle and began to pull, like I'd done hundreds of times before. Numerous times, a giggling girl yelled, "Faster! Faster!" Other times, Jessie clung to her dog and stuffed animals as she soaked up the scenery with her armful of furry friends. I'd answer her questions as I pulled. Jessie always asked questions. On summer days, she would hold her lavender umbrella over her family of critters to shade them from the hot Georgia sun.

Today, however, Jessie's comment caught me off guard. I almost needed to lie down in the wagon (not an easy feat at 6'5") and have Jessie pull me back to the house. How did the tween years get here so quickly? Where did my baby go?

September 22, 2004, 7:56 p.m. The nurse handed me a 7 lb., 10 oz., 20 ½ inches-long, crying baby girl. At age 44 – that's right, forty-four – I was a father. As I held my newborn daughter, her tears became mine. At the time, I didn't realize that more than one new life began a few minutes before eight that Wednesday evening. Three new lives were born – Jessie's, my wife Mattie's, and mine.

Actually, the story began on June 1, 1985, when Mattie and I married. For those readers doing the math, Jessie's arrival took almost 20 years. During this two-decade period, Mattie and I met our educational and career goals. After a 10-year career in banking, Mattie earned her Ph.D. in management and became a college professor. At age 32, I earned my Bachelor's degree in accounting, with a minor in banking and finance, followed by my CPA license a few years later. I guess you could say I've followed a non-traditional path through life … or that I'm slow. During this period, I worked as a banker, accountant, and internal auditor.

Since Jessie's birth, though, I've been Mr. Mom, while Mattie continues to work hard in academia. When Jessie began pre-kindergarten, I decided to pursue a writing career. To date, my syndicated column "MoMENts" has been published in more than 45 regional parenting magazines and newspapers, spanning 21 states and two Canadian provinces. My writings share the joys and challenges of parenthood from the perspective of a stay-at-home dad. Each column ends with a reminder to cherish the moments because time zooms by.

The following pages contain more than 60 stories, including over 50 MoMENts columns, nine award-winning essays, and a story first published in *Not Your Mother's Book ... On Working for a Living*, a nationally distributed anthology series. I organized this book by topic, not chronologically. With a few exceptions, the events described in these stories took place when Jessie was ages 5 through 10.

Back to the neighborhood wagon ride. Jessie and our dog rode back to the house in her red wagon, as I was able to convince Jessie – this time – that it's not embarrassing for a girl to let her dad pull her around the neighborhood. I emphasized, "I'm sure there are lots of girls who wish their dads would be home to take them for wagon rides." As I neared our driveway, I couldn't help but think this could be one of the last times I would get to pull Jessie in her wagon. As much as I look forward to seeing who she will be as a young woman, I will miss my little girl. I made sure to cherish each step until it was time to unload my passengers.

I hope you will enjoy the moments shared in the pages that follow. As you do, perhaps you will be reminded to cherish the time with the children in your life, delight in reminiscing about past experiences, or look forward to fun times yet to come.

Note:

I used nicknames for my family members to protect their anonymity early in the writing process. I have kept these names for continuity.

Chapter 1

A Job Like No Other

I had a successful 20-year professional career in banking, accounting, and auditing. During those "bring home a check" days, I interacted with different types of people and experienced a little bit of everything. My relationships with my coworkers were always the best part of my job, but I also had daily contact with customers.

As a bank branch manager, I made customers happy when I approved their loan requests. Conversely, others left my office disappointed and grumbling when I had to decline their applications. Who wouldn't enjoy playing with money for a living? I counted hundreds of thousands of dollars during my banking days. OK, the fact the money belonged to the bank and not me took away a bit of zest from the experience.

Later, I earned my college diploma as a nontraditional student. Not afraid of grueling experiences, obtaining a CPA license was next on my list. I can't say the four killer tax seasons were the highlight of my professional career: Get up and be on the job before sunrise. Work. Drink lots of coffee. Work. Drink lots of soda. Work. Go home in the dark. Kiss wife, sleep, and begin the process all over again. This described the first quarter of each year, a time when I romanced the coffee maker and soda machine more than my wife, Mattie. The dialogue with Mattie consisted more of groans and grunts than cohesive sentences. However, tax seasons always ended with a big party, and the rest of the year was more conducive to a happy marriage.

The groans and grunts continued after I switched careers again and became an internal auditor at a university. Usually, though, the noises came from the clients I audited. No one likes to see the auditor coming, so I didn't always feel the love. One client even nicknamed me "Columbo," as I always seemed to have another question.

Then, in 2004, Mattie gave birth to our beautiful daughter, Jessie. At age 44, I began yet another new job, this time as a stay-at-home dad. No, I didn't bring home a paycheck, but I didn't sit on the sofa and eat bonbons either. Nearly 10 years later, I can safely say being a stay-at-home dad has been the most demanding, and most rewarding, of my four jobs – without question.

Does it pay well? Not in dollars and cents, but in a lifetime of memories. How do the hours compare? Sixty to 80 hours per week during tax seasons were a piece of cake compared to the 24/7 rigors of Mr. Mom-hood. What noises do I hear? Oh, there have been plenty of comments of displeasure, and groans and grunts, as in my previous jobs. There has also been considerably more crying and a greater variety of fits, and I haven't even reached Jessie's teenage years. With that said, I wouldn't trade a single minute of my past 10 years watching Jessie grow from baby to toddler to almost a tween.

The job of an at-home dad never gets boring, either. Each day, I wear numerous hats, some at the same time. Stay-at-home parenting requires not only the ability to multitask, but also the capacity to deal with ambiguous, rapidly changing conditions. I knock out some chores with no problem, while others require a bit more persistence. But I'm a patient guy by nature. However, although some tasks go as planned, other seemingly simple undertakings quickly turn precarious and can be more difficult to predict than a customer's likelihood of defaulting on a loan.

When Jessie was three years old, she took Kindermusik classes at our church, and she always enjoyed them. I did, too, as Jessie was happy, learning, and having fun. It didn't matter that I was the only man who was clapping, singing, jumping, and holding hands with the rest of the Kindermusik moms and kids. I'm sure my tenor voice stood out on more than one occasion.

Jessie's Kindermusik class immediately preceded my evening tennis league. Being a good planner, I dressed in my tennis shorts, shirt and sneakers, packed my racket and water bottle, and headed directly to the courts as soon as the class ended. Mattie met me at the courts and took Jessie home.

On this particular day, Jessie and I rode up the church elevator with a little boy in the class and his mom. I wore a white T-shirt and gray tennis shorts. The string that supplemented the elastic waist on my shorts had come out in the laundry. I didn't see a need to throw away the shorts as they still fit nicely, so I continued wearing them, minus the string.

As the elevator started moving up, Jessie reached over to hold on to me. Unintentionally, she grabbed my shorts pockets from both sides and before I knew it, my stringless shorts were down below my knees. I yelled, "Jessie!" with only a jockstrap covering my assets. My T-shirt provided no help. Speechless and highly embarrassed, I quickly pulled up my shorts.

The mother in the elevator, who I'm sure saw my red face, along with a whole lot more of me, tried to put me at ease. She told me, "Oh, my son has pulled my blouse down on more than one occasion."

As a "bean counter," I only had to worry about debits and credits, not exposing myself to the public. Let's face it – all jobs are like an elevator. They all have their ups and downs.

When Jessie began Pre-K, I decided to pursue a writing career while continuing to tackle the responsibilities of a stay-at-home parent. So far so good, except for the time I fell out of my desk chair and sprained my ankle . . . but that's another story.

I'll keep working hard to have a successful career while remaining a positive and often-present force in Jessie's life. I'm sure lots of exciting roles are in my future, like being a driver's education instructor and intimidating potential suitors. I plan to sign a few book deals, too.

Of course, I'll be putting out the "fires" each day as a stay-at-home parent. Just the other night, I accidentally stepped on Jessie's doll and broke her leg. I superglued it back in place. I'm not making any guarantees on how long it will stay fastened, but I know when I handed Jessie her doll with two attached legs, her smile was worth a million dollars.

I love this job . . . especially when the sounds I hear are giggles, I'm fully clothed, and each of Jessie's dolls has two legs.

Note: This story was first published in *Not Your Mother's Book ... On Working for a Living.*

Father's Day 2009

Chapter 2

MoMENts of Learning

Class in session – Oprah Winfrey said, "I am a woman in process. I'm just trying like everybody else. I try to take every conflict, every experience, and learn from it. Life is never dull."

I could say the same thing, except I'm a man, a Mr. Mom, in process. My last 10 years as a stay-at-home dad have been filled with learning through all kinds of experiences. I've played the roles of both teacher and student. But whether I'm vacuuming glitter off the dog or sharing my bed with a donkey, a monkey, and a cow, one thing is certain: parenting is a journey of discovery.

"Push the Button!"

Nurse! Minutes earlier, my newborn daughter had been wheeled from the nursery into our hospital room. Nurse, where did you go? Where's the instruction manual? But the nurse was gone.

"Uh, Mattie, I know you just had a C-section, but I need your help here."

These were my thoughts when faced with my first dad challenge – changing Jessie's diaper. The details are still as vivid as the day it happened.

I carefully peeled away the tape on each side of Jessie's diaper. I pulled the diaper away from her belly like a bomb specialist deactivating a live bomb. I must not have been careful enough though, as the "bomb" had exploded. In my 44 years of life, I had never seen anything like it. It turns out that babies' first poops are meconium, a mixture of bile, mucus, and amniotic fluid. I should have paid closer attention in Health class. Let's just say it's not pretty. With Mattie still immobilized by the epidural in her back, solving this problem was all up to me.

I went through a mental checklist of my three careers to draw on my relevant expertise. Twelve years in banking? No, making a loan wouldn't help here. I did have experience in collections. No, not quite the same kind of collections. Four years in public accounting? Debits equal credits. No good. Assets = Liabilities +

Owner's Equity. No help. Cash inflow versus outflow. There was outflow alright, but not cash outflow (although that happened when we received the hospital bills). How about my five years as an internal auditor and investigator? I didn't need to do much investigating to find the guilty party. Based on what I was looking at, Jessie didn't have a good grasp of internal controls.

Luckily, I remembered my Associate's degree in Management. This situation needed to be managed by a strong leader. I needed a plan. Plan A: I could do the 25-yard dash down to the nurse's station and announce, "Emergency! Emergency!" No, I have my pride.

Plan B: I could calmly strut down the hall to the nurse's station and request a little assistance. No, I was way past the "calmly strutting" stage.

Plan C: I could push the button on the remote on Mattie's bed to signal the nurse's station.

Our first parenting disagreement ensued when I informed Mattie that we needed to call the nurse. She said "You can't call the nurse for a dirty diaper!" Undeterred, I sprinted from Jessie's bassinet to the remote hanging on the side of Mattie's hospital bed. The nurse arrived within seconds. She smiled and said I wasn't the first dad to push the button. Diaper Changing 101 followed.

There have been numerous times over the past six years as a stay-at-home dad when I wished I could have simply "pushed the button" for assistance. Something tells me I'm in for many more button-pushing situations.

Happy Reading

National Read Across America Day is held annually on March 2, the birthday of Dr. Seuss. My daughter has read just about all of Dr. Seuss' books.

Jessie loves to read. When it's time to begin her homework, she always does her reading first. However, getting her to tackle her spelling homework is a challenge. I think she'd rather clean her room, give up dessert, or even the dreaded "take a nap," than knock out her spelling assignment.

One of the reasons why Jessie loves to read may be that for more than five years, I've taken her to our local library for "Reading to Rover." This program really gets kids excited about reading. Children read books to therapy dogs while the dogs' handlers look on and offer help or encouragement. Jessie has read to all kinds of dogs – huge ones and tiny ones, purebreds and mixed breeds. The kids enjoy petting the dogs, and reading to them is more fun and less intimidating than reading to people.

Monday evening, as I watched Jessie read to a beautiful German shepherd, I remembered when she was a toddler, sitting in my lap on the floor, petting the dogs while I read. I always kept one eye on her to make sure she didn't grab a fistful of fur. As she grew older, I sat on the floor beside her while she read simple picture books to the dogs. Now I watch from a nearby chair as she nestles up next to the dog, petting it while she reads at a speed that is probably faster than the dog can comprehend.

Inspired by Monday's visit to the library, Jessie devised a way to read to Sadie, our 14-week-old puppy who doesn't like to sit still. Jessie dug out her kindergarten nap mat and put it on the kitchen floor. Then, determined to keep Sadie on the mat while reading to her, she put Sadie on a leash and tied the leash to the refrigerator door. The plan worked and Sadie kept Jessie company as she read the whole chapter book. We're hoping Sadie will eventually become one of the great therapy dogs at Reading to Rover. Jessie is taking steps to ensure that Sadie will be ready, even if the library implements a dress code someday. She dresses Sadie in a variety of outfits and accessories, most recently a flowing blond wig. If you see a sheltie puppy walking down the street wearing a cheerleading costume, three necklaces, and a hair bow, it's probably ours.

We all realize the importance of reading well. Many sources contribute to a child's reading proficiency – parents, grandparents, teachers, and even therapy dogs and their handlers. So, as we approach another Read Across America Day, take a minute to thank those who help children learn to read.

Before leaving the library Monday evening, my passionate reader checked out more than a dozen books to read at home. Now if only I could get a therapy dog for spelling. Come to think of it, maybe I have one. Jessie set a new speed record for finishing her spelling homework when I told her that, if there was time left before bed, she could take a bath with Sadie. I may be on to something. This could work for math, too. I just might end up with the cleanest dog in town.

$3.84

Note: I wrote this column in August 2011 during the Great Recession, when the housing market collapsed.

HOUSE FOR SALE! My family and I moved to Statesboro, Georgia in July, 2007. Unfortunately, our house in Seneca, South Carolina is still for sale. For readers who are doing the math, that's over four years. To say it's been a big disappointment to watch our property's value decline year after year after year after year is a mild understatement. Does anyone want to buy a great house in South Carolina at a very good price?

In the summer of 2009, our house had been on the market for about 18 months. Although we had dropped the price four times, it remained unsold. I drove up to check on the house and clean it, as I had been doing every 6-8 weeks since we moved. On that particular trip, however, I discovered some water damage. The next couple of days were stressful. On the 215-mile return trip to Statesboro, I was tired, frustrated, and feeling a little sorry for myself ... okay, feeling a lot sorry for myself. I did not need this extra repair challenge and another cash outflow on a house that was losing its value faster than I could reduce its asking price.

The Saturday night after I returned, I took Jessie – then four years old – out on a daddy-daughter date. She had wanted to try the Dairy Queen restaurant ever since we moved to Statesboro. Jessie ordered "a banana split to share with my daddy, please." I paid the $3.84 tab and we went to our table to anxiously wait for our first father-daughter banana split.

When it arrived, Jessie scooped the strawberry, pineapple, and chocolate toppings into her mouth. She left me the plain vanilla ice cream and banana. That's how Mattie shares ice cream sundaes, too, so perhaps Jessie inherited the tendency. That one banana split helped me put everything back in perspective. My little girl was as happy as she could be. She said "yum yum" at least three times, and she was not nearly as quiet about it as I would have preferred.

Prior to that banana split, I felt frazzled from worrying about the house and frustrated about its declining value. I only had to spend $3.84. Jessie's face said the rest with a smile wider than the banana in her sundae. Life is great!

As of this writing, our house is still for sale. We have now reduced the price eight times. Last year, a tree fell on it, resulting in a quick trip to Seneca and an additional cash outflow. Did I ask if anyone wants to buy a great house in South Carolina?

I'm sure everything will work out with our house. In the meantime, we had a fabulous time at La'berry on Sunday. I even got to have some toppings with my frozen yogurt (Jessie and I had separate bowls). Life is great!

Update: The house sold in July 2013. It was on the market for six years.

The Joy of Writing … and Remembering

Mattie has many strengths. Remembering important dates is not one of them. November 15, 2011 will be the 30th anniversary of our first date. Will she remember? The odds aren't great.

November 15 isn't just our anniversary, though. It's also the 10th anniversary of "I Love to Write Day," celebrated in nine states "to have people of all ages spend time writing."

I enjoy writing. I write teasing notes to make Mattie laugh. When she travels for work, I send her long emails with details of how Jessie and I spent our day. For birthdays and special occasions, I make personalized "Hempmark" cards. On our anniversaries, I'll often write a note with the date on it, to see if it reminds Mattie … it usually doesn't.

Jessie enjoys writing, too. She's always making cards, books, or notes documenting her numerous observations and experiments. Mattie and I help her keep a journal of the highlights of each day, which has improved Jessie's writing skills. It has also helped us to understand Jessie better, because we learn what she perceives as the best parts of her days.

When she's older, I'm confident Jessie will look back through her journals and remember the wonderful times and loved ones who touched her life. She may smile when she sees her journals go from print to cursive, from pencil to pen. She might get out her pen and add punctuation marks; a number of her sentences end without any, something her parents and teachers have been trying to correct.

Even though keeping the journals has been excellent writing practice, and Mattie and I followed-up on some of her entries with unwelcome grammar or spelling lessons, she'll be glad she took time to write. The journals will help her recall the ways she spent her childhood, both the ordinary moments and the special occasions.

In an effort to enhance my own writing skills, I attended the annual Southeastern Writers Association workshop this past June. Near the end of the five-day conference, participants read a one-page sample of their writing, and a literary agent and two published authors judged them in a contest modeled after a reality-TV show. When the judges heard something they didn't like, they raised their hands. If two judges raised their hands, you were done. Then they provided constructive feedback.

I stayed up well past midnight preparing for the contest and went to bed confident I had written four of the greatest paragraphs ever typed. My illusion ended after two paragraphs. Ouch! Okay, that hurt, but to paraphrase John Paul Jones, "I have not yet begun to write!"

John Riddle, founder of "I Love to Write Day," points out "when people become stronger writers, they become better communicators." Communicating well strengthens relationships, and we all want good relationships. So, I'm encouraging my readers to participate. Write a note and put it in a loved one's lunch, or on the refrigerator or bathroom mirror. Write a letter to a friend or family member (Mattie, please don't write anything for my already long Honey-Do list). Write a love letter to your spouse or a letter of thanks (Mattie, feel free to write one of these to me).

What will I be doing on November 15? I'm going to share "I Love to Write Day" with Jessie's first-grade class. I can't wait to see what they write. I just hope when I share my writing with them, they let me read more than the first two paragraphs! I'll also be wishing Mattie happy 30th anniversary of our first date, and chances are pretty good she'll be getting a love letter. Unfortunately, it's also likely that before she opens the envelope, she'll look up at me and ask, "What's this for?"

The Wonders Ahead

Jessie recently introduced me to the "Eighth Wonder of the World." Who would have thought we'd find it at a Golden Corral in Florida.

Chocolate flows from a big fountain at the restaurant's dessert bar. Patrons use skewers to pick up strawberries, pineapples, marshmallows, or whatever else they choose to dip into the cascade of chocolate. Golden Corral calls it the "Chocolate Wonderfall" and promotes it as the "Eighth Wonder of the World." Walking back from the dessert bar with her eyes wide open and a big smile, Jessie certainly looked as if she had just seen the "eighth wonder." Before long, chocolate surrounded her mouth. It tasted so good that her shirt ate some, too.

"What are the seven wonders of the world?" Whoops. I should have anticipated that question. Jessie always has questions, and I knew I didn't have the answer to that one. Google frequently helps me with answers; however, my computer was locked in the car. I thought about saying, "Just enjoy your chocolate-covered fruit," but I always try my best to answer Jessie's questions. I could only remember the pyramids of Giza.

As I researched the answer later, I learned that numerous "seven wonders" lists have been created. I was thinking of the Seven Wonders of the Ancient World.

I'm not really concerned with ancient wonders, though, but future ones, the wonders that lie ahead for

Jessie. It's exciting to see how she views things through her young eyes. Little experiences are magnified. A stream of chocolate sauce is as impressive as Niagara Falls. Her logic differs from that of her parents, too. For example, we allowed Jessie a second dessert after her chocolate-covered fruit and marshmallow. She chose a slice of carrot cake. With the most serious look on her face, she told Mattie and me, "The vegetable of the day is carrots, so I chose carrot cake."

I'll always cherish the wonders of Jessie's first seven years – her first snow, her first banana split, her first trip to Disney, and so many more. The wonders have never needed to be colossal like a great pyramid. Yesterday, she called me from her grandparents' house to tell me that she had found a Canadian quarter. She described it as if she had located a lost treasure chest of rubies and diamonds. The wonders haven't had to cost a lot of money either, though a banana split is certainly cheaper than a trip to Disney World. Many of the wonders didn't even require a lot of time. "Dad, come look at this giant worm!" It was worthy of several photographs and a video of it crawling across the sidewalk. "Dad, baby birds are in our birdhouse!" Even seeing the Chick-fil-A cow was once a moo-ving experience.

How many wonders lie ahead for Jessie ... hundreds, thousands? Many of these will also be wonders for Mattie and me. A few weeks ago, I stood with Jessie as she bounced with excitement while waiting in line to go down her first big waterslide. Though I've slid down many waterslides in my lifetime, until then I never went down one head-first. It was a wonder-fall experience!

I'm really glad I got to witness Jessie enjoy the "eighth wonder," too, and not just because it was mighty tasty. Now if I can only get her to see vegetables as wonders.

Learning to Chill

I don't enjoy packing for trips. In fact, I'd almost rather have my dentist fix a cavity without novocaine. Don't ask me how I managed to squeeze a high chair, stroller, and playpen into the van, along with the rest of our luggage, during Jessie's baby years. I must admit that packing is a lot easier without that stuff. Jessie is 8 now, so the most important piece of luggage is her "entertainment" suitcase – books, crayons, colored pencils, gel pens, paper, glue, scissors, and markers. Jessie's bottles of glitter remain at home, always. To be honest, I wouldn't be disappointed if they stayed in her art drawer, always.

Wikipedia defines *glitter* as "an assortment of very small pieces of copolymer plastics, aluminum foil, titanium dioxide, iron oxides, bismuth oxychloride or other materials painted in metallic, neon and iridescent colors to reflect light in a sparkling spectrum." I have my own definition, but I think it's best not to put it in print. Let's just say I'm not a big fan.

On the other hand, Jessie can't wait to do art projects using glitter. I enjoy watching her create things with Play-Doh. I applaud the masterpieces she paints on her easel. I even smile when she pulls out her assorted containers of glue, even though I know my fingers will end up sticking to something before all is said and done. But oh, those very small pieces of copolymer plastics ....

31

I learned that machinist Henry Ruschmann in 1934 invented a way to grind up plastics to make large quantities of glitter. He founded Meadowbrook Inventions, still a major supplier of the substance. Its slogan is, "Our glitter covers the world." I can't verify the accuracy of the slogan, but I can attest that by the time Jessie finishes using it, glitter covers our house.

Although I will never win a Good Housekeeping award for having the cleanest house, I do like to keep a tidy one. I'd give myself good grades for cleaning, except for dusting, where I'd be happy with a C-. My wife and I were married over 19 years before Jessie came along. It was a lot easier to keep things tidy (and glitter-free) back then.

When I compare our 19 years as a couple to the eight years we've been a family of three (four really, with the dog), I have happy memories of both periods that I wouldn't trade for anything. The status of the house (tidy or a mess) is not too important. That doesn't mean I don't need to take a few extra breaths when it seems like I'm taking one step forward and two steps back as I attempt to keep the house in order. I guess you could say I'm "learning to chill."

Jessie just finished making an eight-page, glitter-filled activity book at the kitchen table. She had so much fun working on this project as she drew ovals on the pages with glue, then buried them with glitter. Right now, glitter is everywhere – the table, chairs, floor, her clothing, and the dog. Even though I'll vacuum the entire work area, including Jessie, glitter will somehow find its way into every room of the house. The "pre-chilled" dad would moan and groan. However, the "post-chilled" dad sees the sparkle in his child's eyes, along with various places on her face and body, as she shows off her book. So thank you, Mr. Ruschmann, for your shimmery invention. But, a bigger thanks goes out to the inventor of the vacuum cleaner.

Jessie prepared her activity book to take on an upcoming trip. She says it will make the time pass faster in the car. I praised Jessie for her creative idea and for taking responsibility for her own entertainment. However, that glitter-dripping book isn't going anywhere near the family van. I guess I haven't fully mastered the art of "chilling."

Manatees Aren't Fat

One of my daily highlights is to walk 8-year-old Jessie to her classroom. I kiss the top of her head and tell her to have a good day. However, today's morning routine varied. It was a typical drive to school as we practiced a few spelling words for the day's test. As Jessie exited the van, she did a spin in her dress and a ballet jump in the parking lot. Nothing new there.

When we entered the building, she saw one of her male classmates and shouted, "Manatees aren't fat!" Apparently, she has a friendly feud with a few boys in her class about the weight issues of manatees. Still nothing out of the ordinary from my independent, free-spirited girl. Then, she pulled her book bag from my hand and slung it over her shoulder as she sped to her classroom a few steps ahead of me. I quickly questioned, "Don't you want a kiss?" She turned around and said, "I'm fine," and off into her classroom she went, happy to start another day. Jessie may have been fine, but I was not. It was a long walk back to the car.

As I drove home, I thought about what I had heard on the radio a day earlier. The disc jockey reported that 6- to 15-year-olds were asked in a survey, "Who do you turn to for advice?" I sure would have hoped the number one answer was Mom and Dad. A few seconds later, the disc jockey said it wasn't parents. I guessed "friends" next. Nope. Grandparents? Wrong again. Church leaders? Uh-uh. It turns out they turn to Google for advice. Google!

This has the makings of a challenging day. First, I don't get my morning kiss, and now my daughter's going to turn to the computer for advice instead of her dad. What will Jessie type into Google? "Should I let a boy hold my hand?" I can answer that one. "When should dads stop kissing their children?" I can handle that one, too – Never! "Should I hop on the back of a motorcycle if invited?" Again, an easy answer for me. I apologize to my motorcycle-riding readers in advance, but I don't want Jessie driving 70 miles per hour down the highway on a motorcycle with her arms wrapped around some guy's waist. Ever.

After thinking about this for a while, I remembered how often Jessie asks me a question and I say, "I don't know. Let's Google it."

Okay, so maybe Google and I can co-exist, but not when it comes to select topics. It could be useful, though, for questions like, "Are manatees fat?" I Googled it. According to one site, manatees eat a lot of food with low nutritional value, but have little body fat, which is why they don't like cold water. So, to the boys in Jessie's class, "My girl was right." But more important, I see advantages to having Google close by, especially if I can search for answers while Jessie sleeps and be prepared with brilliant responses in the morning.

I told Jessie about the survey results shared by the radio disc jockey. She wasn't surprised. "Mom and Dad are always here for you," I emphasized, "and you can always come to us for advice." I also told Jessie that I Googled manatees and she was right, but that I only checked one site, and it's important to review several credible sources because you can't believe everything you read. She responded, "That's okay. It proves I'm right, so you don't need to check further." Jessie asked me to make a printout of the website for her Show-and-Tell tomorrow.

I'm glad Jessie is independent and free-spirited. No matter what the future holds, something tells me she'll be able to handle the boys just fine, as well as other life challenges that come her way. As for me, I know one day I'll hear, "Dad, you don't need to walk me to class." "I want to get my driver's license." "I'm leaving for college now."

I just might have to turn to Google for advice.

Pink Bunny

Friday nights are for high school football, not bunny-sitting. It's 8 p.m. on a Friday. I'm lying on the sofa holding a pink stuffed bunny. My left leg is elevated by three pillows and an ice pack surrounds my ankle. Earlier today, I suffered my first writer's injury. That's right, a writer's injury. Don't fall out of your chair laughing, because that's how I landed in this predicament. Not the laughing part, the falling out of the chair part.

I had safe working conditions throughout my 20-year professional career. Who knew I would have to worry about injuries as I pursue my dream of becoming a successful writer? After all, what are the risks? A broken fingernail or two? Come to think of it, eye strain, carpel tunnel, and neck or back pain from bending over a keyboard for hours are other risks. Maybe I need to consider a different career?

My fall occurred early this afternoon. I had been typing for quite some time, sitting with my legs crossed and back hunched. As I stood up from my chair, my ankle twisted. I hit the floor faster than an editor can throw one of my manuscripts onto a slush pile. For the record, I do not drink alcohol while I write. Apparently, my left foot had fallen asleep and I didn't realize it until I put weight on it.

Although twisting my ankle hurt, the pain subsided. I took a test walk around the house, then picked up Jessie from school. We went directly to her friend's birthday party, where I had a good time watching her play laser tag. However, as I sat down to watch her bowl, my ankle began to throb. When I stood up, I couldn't put any weight on my left foot. I limped through the rest of the party and then hobbled out to the parking lot.

I had planned to take Jessie to the football game this evening, but with my ankle now swollen and in serious pain, it wasn't possible. What excuse could I offer Jessie? "Jessie, your dad twisted his ankle getting out of his chair." See what I mean? I needed to come up with something to save my pride.

I quickly thought of possible explanations. "One of the boys at the party dropped a bowling ball on my foot" or "I tripped while watching you shoot lasers in the dark arena." Since I had played tennis the night before, I guess I could have gone with, "I twisted my ankle last night and it's just starting to bother me now." Any one of these explanations had to be better than a "writing injury."

Perhaps I could tell her the truth about falling out of my chair, but exaggerate the details surrounding the fall. "I spilled hot coffee on my lap." Too bad I don't drink coffee. Since our dog, Ginger, rests beside my chair, I could say, "I rolled the desk chair back and ran over Ginger's paw, resulting in the clumsy exit from my chair when she yelped." Plausible, except I had the limp, not Ginger.

I decided to go with the truth, just like Mattie and I want Jessie to tell us the truth, the whole truth, and nothing but the truth. I may need to rethink this position when Jessie becomes a teenager, as I'm not sure I'll be tough enough to handle the whole truth. Okay, then she should tell just her mom the whole truth.

When we returned from the birthday party, I limped into the house and plopped down on the sofa. A daddy-daughter date to the football game turned into a mommy-daughter event.

Before they left, Jessie and Mattie helped me to get comfortable. Jessie pulled an ice pack from the freezer. She applied direct pressure to my ankle with the ice pack. Grimacing, I told her that this might not be the best remedy. She disagreed and continued with her rehabilitation plan. Mattie retrieved three pillows to elevate my ankle. Then, Jessie brought me her pink bunny to cap off the "love."

Life is filled with good times and obstacles. When an obstacle – or in my case, the air – knocks you down, you pick yourself up and move on. You can whine and be miserable, or you can try to keep a good attitude. It's okay to laugh at yourself, too. Tonight, those were my lessons for Jessie. I take the teaching moments as they come. Next Friday, Jessie and I will be back in the stands, talking about teamwork and good sportsmanship. I'll leave Pink Bunny at home.

I didn't see any touchdowns this evening. I did type this story from the sofa with Pink Bunny by my side. Though my writing career may be off to a stumbling start, I still think I have promise. In fact, I read this story out loud to Pink Bunny and didn't get a single negative comment.

I'm gaining experience as a writer, too. Heck, I didn't fall off the sofa a single time.

The Gift of Laughter

In mid-May, 9-year-old Jessie and I attended a show at our local theatre. At the end of the performance, the director came on stage to thank people for their support. She concluded, "I hope you all have a nice Christmas." The audience erupted with laughter, at which point she realized her mistake and clarified, "I meant to say have a nice summer."

No matter the season, I love to laugh. It's one of my favorite things to do. When I am the target of the laughter without intending to be, I don't take myself too seriously and laugh right along. This is good, as tired dads, like frazzled show directors, occasionally make humorous mistakes.

For example, Mattie recently wanted to give someone my email address and couldn't remember it. When I told her the address, which began with my last name, I spelled "Hempfing" for her. Mattie gave me an odd look. I said, "What?" Then, it hit me that my wife knows how to spell my last name.

Jessie also fills my life with laughter, even though she sometimes simultaneously frustrates and exhausts me. I love Jessie with all my heart, but she's heard me say many times, "Girl, you wear me out." I've learned I must choose my battles wisely. So, if something minor happens, I try to laugh it off instead of getting upset.

Okay, maybe I stress out just a little. A recent example comes to mind.

Mattie had an overnight trip, so it was just Daddy and daughter on Monday morning. Jessie's third-grade class had a field trip to a farm that day. After breakfast, I told Jessie to go apply sunscreen. After waiting three times as long as it should have taken, I checked on her. She had dutifully applied the sunscreen, but then proceeded to drench her pigtailed hair with Mattie's hairspray. As I stepped toward her for a closer look, she gave it an additional squirt. It was now past time to leave for school, and my daughter's hair looked as wet as if she'd just gotten out of the shower – and I knew it would soon dry to the hardness of her bicycle helmet.

Jessie's morning routine never includes hairspray. A few nights earlier, though, she had performed in a ballet recital and her teacher had used hairspray to secure the girls' buns.

It would have been bad enough to send Jessie to school with only her teacher and classmates to notice her immovable-even-in-gale-force-winds hair, but since it was a field trip day, lots of mothers would be going along. Deep down, I think we all care what other people think, even if we say we don't. I tried not to make a big deal out of Jessie's hair. Shaking my head, I left the room and advised myself, "The girl is just like her independent momma, so let it go."

As I drove my fragrant, shiny-headed daughter to school, I brought up the topic of adequate hairspray usage. Apparently, I can give advice but can't take it, even from myself. Jessie responded, "It's not too much hairspray, Dad. There's high humidity today." I laughed out loud at my daughter's quick thinking and felt relief that the hairspray caking her head hadn't affected her brain. Although we missed the 8 a.m. bell by three minutes, I dropped Jessie off before the late bell, at which point we would have had to go to the office for a tardy slip. Before she exited the van, I reminded her to stay away from fire, as she was highly flammable.

In hindsight, maybe the show director wasn't wrong in wishing everyone a nice Christmas. We all receive gifts throughout the year, and Jessie gives me gifts of laughter every day. I'm going to take time to enjoy her daily gifts. Okay, maybe not all of them.

Last night, Jessie surprised me with a picnic of open-faced mandarin orange sandwiches sprinkled with powdered sugar. I sent my non-appetizing sandwich back to the kitchen, but Jessie ate hers. I asked, "How was it?" She answered, "Not bad, but the bread was soggy" (from the sugary juice that dripped from the canned oranges). What was I to do? I laughed.

A Donkey, a Monkey, and a Cow

Sometimes a good story falls right into my lap … or in this case, jumps into my lap. Before I tell my story, though, I want to share the reasons why I write.

First, it's a way to earn income while keeping a flexible schedule. For example, I'm typing this at 2:30 a.m.

Second, it feels great to brighten someone's day, even if it's just by giving a few minutes of enjoyable reading. I love when readers respond to my columns by sharing happy memories of their own.

Third, time flies by. Mattie recently asked, "Do you realize our *baby* is already halfway to 18?" As I remind readers to "cherish the moments," I'm prompting myself to do the same with Jessie during life's hectic days.

Last, and most important, my writings create a permanent record of the incredible love I hold for Jessie. When she reads the stories in years to come, she'll remember the great times and know how much her parents treasured her. It's time for one of those stories, but be forewarned; one part would be classified as "not great," especially from a male perspective.

I'm a light sleeper. If Jessie calls me from her bedroom on the other side of the house, I'll wake up about 90 percent of the time. Recently, however, one of the 10 percent times occurred. Jessie had a bad dream and called, "Daddy!" When Daddy didn't show up, Jessie decided to run to her parents' bedroom. She brought along her stuffed animals, Eeyore, the donkey, and Sam, short for Samantha, her brown monkey. To summarize, at a few minutes after 1 a.m., an 83-pound frightened girl, toting a monkey and a donkey, ran frantically into the master bedroom and made a flying leap onto her daddy. Still groggy, I tried to calm Jessie.

"Calm down, calm down. It's okay. Calm down before somebody gets hurt!" About three seconds later, that somebody was me, as Jessie's knee landed … well, let's just say had I known this was coming, I would have gone to bed wearing the protective cup I used during my church-softball-playing days.

When Jessie calmed down, she snuggled in between Mattie and me, with one arm around Eeyore and Sam, and fell asleep. Once I'm awake, though, I have a tough time falling back to sleep, especially after being awakened by 83 pounds of blunt force trauma, followed by a swift knee in the groin. I turned over on my side, hoping to catch a few winks. However, instead of finding sleep, I was goosed … by a cow. I erred when I thought Jessie only brought Eeyore and Sam. She had also carried her cow, Cuddles. Thank goodness it wasn't Unicorn.

I knew I wouldn't be falling back to sleep anytime soon, so I left Jessie in bed with Mattie and went to the living room to read, and drifted off in my recliner. Later, I moved to the sofa and slept there before getting up to take the dog for her morning walk.

After a brisk walk, a yawning dad went to wake Jessie for school. As I looked down at my sleeping family, one word came to mind – thankful ("tired" would have worked, too). Jessie had maintained her position in the middle of the bed with Mattie on one side, and Eeyore, Sam, and Cuddles on the other. The three stuffed animals were resting comfortably on my favorite pillow. Cuddles and Sam looked up at me with their stitched smiles. I smiled back.

Sure, Mattie and I had been deprived of a little sleep. However, we had received an opportunity to show Jessie that we are always there for her, to protect, comfort, and love her. Jessie's flying leap reminded me to be thankful for the opportunities I have to make a difference as a dad (though I'd prefer future ones to be pain-free).

This leads me to one final reason why I write. Writing is therapeutic for this sleep-deprived father.

Remember to cherish the moments, even if you're awakened by a bony-kneed kid, goosed by a cow, and lose your favorite pillow to a group of stuffed mammals.

The Scent of a Kitchen

For Valentine's Day 2013, Jessie and I baked a pound cake for my wife, Mattie. I remember it well because I'm not sure if the kitchen has recovered. I'm pretty sure I haven't. Egg slime ran down the cabinet. I fished egg shells from the batter. Flour dust covered the dish detergent bottle, faucet, and coffee pot. Jessie melted butter until it boiled over in the microwave. Luckily, I heard the splatter and stopped the microwave; three minutes remained on the timer.

Even a little bit of vanilla extract left on a teaspoon proved problematic. Jessie asked, "May I have it?" She made a face after she licked the teaspoon. Apparently, vanilla smells better than it tastes. Ten minutes later, Jessie complained of a bellyache. Little did I realize, my head would soon ache.

Jessie had used the hand-held electric mixer to stir the ingredients. I asked her to hand me the mixer so I could make sure the batter was well mixed, but we had a poor exchange. Fumble! The mixer, turning at full speed, plopped into the bowl. Batter sprayed everywhere – my shirt, my pants, the wall, the sink, the coffee maker. Jessie avoided the erupting batter by running into the living room.

Had I remained calm, I would have unplugged the cord from the outlet, but one doesn't think well while his kitchen, and self, are being painted in batter. I pulled the mixer from the remaining ingredients in the bowl, careful not to get my fingers caught in the spinning beaters, thereby ending my writing career.

Jessie came back into the kitchen as clean-up began. She retrieved a spatula to scrape the batter that blanketed the mixer back into the bowl. Surprisingly, enough batter remained and before too long, the sweet aroma of pound cake filled the kitchen.

Next, Jessie wanted to help with the Valentine's Day supper. She suggested I cut the onions and chicken while she peeled the potatoes. After thinking, "I don't have energy to clean up blood," I gave her permission. While Jessie peeled the potatoes, she sang "Over the Rainbow." As my fatigued head rested against the kitchen cabinets, my beautiful girl wished upon a star.

Jessie still loves to bake, cook, and microwave. On a recent Saturday when Mattie was out of town, Jessie and I were watching my favorite college football team hold onto a one-point lead. Jessie turned to me and said, "I'm hungry." I said, "I am, too." Jessie quickly responded, "I'll make supper." Since my team needed me to cheer them on, I said, "Okay, but don't burn down the house."

Jessie cut a hard-boiled egg in half and delivered it in a glass bowl. Then she heated a can of chicken soup on the stove and served it. All was going well, but then I picked up an all-too-familiar scent – the smell of something burning. I opted to run to the kitchen and forget about my team nursing their one-point lead.

"What's burning?!"

"Everything's okay, Dad. Please don't look." Jessie likes to surprise me. Trust me; if I smell something burning, I'm going to look.

Jessie had over-microwaved two cookies. She served me the blackened one with a scoop of mint chocolate chip ice cream on the side and covered the burnt cookie with chocolate syrup and white chocolate morsels.

As I enjoyed my dessert, I asked Jessie, "Did you turn off the stove?" Jessie ran into the kitchen. I heard the stove knob click, followed by, "It's off now."

My team held on for a one-point victory. When I read the sports page the next morning, the kitchen still smelled like burnt cookie.

What did I learn from these experiences? Wear an apron – always. Chocolate syrup is a good condiment for burnt desserts. Though I enjoy college football, I cherish living in my house more. Most important, I must continue to let Jessie try things so she can grow ... but with supervision.

I don't know what Valentine's Day 2016 will bring, but I plan to keep a scented candle on hand. If I don't use it to mask the smell of burnt food, it can always provide a romantic ambience for my valentine.

Chapter 3

MoMENts of Time Passing Quickly

Hold on – Last night, Jessie's school held a dance for second through fifth graders. Jessie painted her fingernails and toenails purple to match her dress. She applied makeup, too, and asked me if her hair looked good. Before I drove her to school, I took a few pictures of the beautiful, grown-up young lady who had somehow taken over the body of the baby her mom and I brought home from the hospital.

When we arrived, Jessie said, "Dad, you can just drop me off at the door. You don't need to come in. I'm 10."

Wow! Some hectic days, I'm so tired I can barely hold on until Jessie is tucked into bed. Other times, like this one, I want to pick up my little girl, hold her, and never let go.

After the drop-off, I came home and picked up Sadie, our 22-pound dog, and cradled her in my arms. Needless to say, though I love my dog, I didn't feel the same connection as with my baby daughter. I don't think Sadie enjoyed it all that much either.

Dream Big

Each fall, we turn the clock back one hour. Wouldn't it be interesting if we could turn the clock back a month, a year, 35 years? I'm sure we would all make a different decision or two if given the opportunity for do-overs. I wish I had gone out for my high school's basketball team. Unfortunately, I will never realize the dream of playing for a basketball championship. But I can, and do, dream other dreams. I also enjoy sharing in the dreams of my daughter.

Last fall when I spoke with Jessie's first-grade class about writing, I held up my first rejection letter from a publisher. I talked about the importance of setting goals and not quitting when things become difficult.

I then showed the class a copy of Dr. Seuss' book *To Think That I Saw It on Mulberry Street,* his first children's book. Though it was rejected at least 27 times, he didn't give up. Millions of lives have been enriched by *Green Eggs and Ham, The Cat in the Hat,* and *The Grinch who Stole Christmas* because he didn't abandon his goals when they became difficult. I ended my talk by reminding the kids to "Dream Big."

I then asked the class to make a book. Each child would be the author and illustrator for one page. I held up a cover page titled "Our Biggest Dreams" and asked the kids to write at least one sentence and draw a picture to go with it.

For the next 25 minutes, the kids tackled this project with enthusiasm. As they shared their dreams in words and pictures, I learned that Jessie's class was full of kids who wanted to invent. One girl wanted to make a flying robot that could clean up her room. Other kids dreamed of inventing a flying motorcycle, a new car, a new school, and a new type of computer. Some children wanted to have exciting jobs, such as being a soccer player, working at Disney World, and being an astronaut. Still others dreamed of helping animals by becoming an animal rescuer or a vet. One boy wrote 14 sentences. I think he might become an author.

As parents, our most important dreams are those we have for our children. We want them to dream big dreams and have opportunities to achieve them. It's tempting for parents to try to live their lost dreams through their children.

Jessie inherited my height and could be a future basketball star. I could live vicariously through her. I've come to realize, though, that imposing my dreams on her isn't the best solution. Nevertheless, we still practice shooting, passing, and dribbling in the driveway. I take her to tennis lessons, too. Yet, Jessie will dream her own dreams, and Mattie and I will be there to support her. So far, she's wanted to be a college professor, a vet, own and manage a Walmart, and teach braille to the blind.

Since I can't turn the clock back more than one hour a year, I will focus my attention forward. I will continue to have dreams for myself and pursue my own goals. One day I will show one of my own books, instead of a rejection letter, when I speak to a class of children about the joys of writing. It will be a New York Times bestseller, too. And, when Jessie's classmate invents a flying robot that can clean a house, I'm buying one.

Little in the Middle

Where did my little baby go? I was just rocking Jessie, holding her in one arm and singing lullabies. Now it takes two hands, an inhale, and a grunt to lift her.

A few months ago, my wife's uncle came for an overnight visit. He slept in Jessie's room, and she slept in the master bedroom with Mattie and me. In the past when we've had guests stay in Jessie's room, she has slept in a sleeping bag on the floor of our room. This time, however, I thought of Billy Dean's *Let Them Be Little*, and decided to let Jessie sleep between her mom and me in our king-size bed. I thought there would be plenty of room, failing to take into account that Jessie would bring her pillow, her butterfly Pillow Pet, and her stuffed animals – Eeyore, Cuddles, Panda, Sealie, Giraffee, Amanda, and Armadillo. I hadn't realized I'd be sleeping at the zoo.

Let's just say it wasn't the best night of sleep I've ever had. Jessie and Mattie were asleep by the time I got to bed. I gently pushed Jessie toward the middle of the bed and relocated a few of her stuffed animals. All 10 of us were now in bed. This would have been fine except Jessie is a "flopper." She twisted and repositioned herself throughout the night. One time she kicked me so hard, I thought she had to be dreaming about sports. If I was the football and she was the field goal kicker, the kick would have been good from forty yards out. In contrast to me,

Jessie apparently had a fine night's sleep. When she woke up, she told Mattie, "Daddy didn't even come to bed last night."

I'm still touched by the song *Let Them Be Little;* its lyrics share a powerful message to love and support our children, and enjoy their childhood with them. I play it sometimes to remind myself to make the most of my time with Jessie while she is still young, and to take time for the everyday activities that are fun for a little kid. As for sleeping in the middle, though, once was enough. I'll choose to sleep on the sofa the next time we have overnight guests.

This morning, I gave Mattie a hug in front of the kitchen sink. When Jessie sees hugs, she yells "Family hug!" and runs to join in. So even though our "sleeping in the middle" days are over, family hugs with Jessie squeezed between her mom and me have no age limit.

Staying Young

Do children keep you young? Ask me in 10 years when Jessie is 17, and I'll probably say no and blame my gray hair – if I have any left – on worrying about her driving and her plans to leave for college. At least I won't lose my youth by worrying about boys, because she's not allowed to date until she's 29.

Sometimes Jessie makes me feel young. I've done things with her I haven't done in years, like playing jacks, pick-up sticks, and hopscotch. Don't laugh; I had a big sister! I also get to try lots of new things, like waiting in long lines at Disney for autographs of princesses and fairies. I can hold my own in jump-rope competitions, too. So I'm staying young, right? It doesn't always feel that way.

When Jessie was 5 years old, Mattie and I took her to a school dance. Jessie had a fantastic time jumping up and down to the music. I, however, had mixed emotions. On one hand, I was happy that Jessie had so much fun with her friends. On the other hand, I felt old. Make that ancient. I hadn't expected to hear a lot of Barry Manilow or Air Supply, but I was shocked I didn't recognize more than a handful of songs. I actually enjoyed listening to *Rocky Top* because it was familiar, even though I normally find it distressing. I'm an avid Florida Gators football fan and their rival, University of Tennessee, plays *Rocky Top* after every touchdown.

During the dance, I could tell from the decibel level of the screams that Justin Bieber songs, especially *Baby* and *U Smile,* were the kids' favorites. I left the dance knowing I had fallen way behind with today's music. I set out to catch up so I could be a more in-touch father. For starters, I bought Jessie the Justin Bieber CD she wanted. We listen to it together when we have picnics in the yard or garage. I've also let her use my computer to play some of the songs she hears at school, and I pay close attention. As she listens, she invents all kinds of dances. For now, I'm focusing on becoming hip with the music — my dance moves can wait. I can't say my efforts have really helped, though. I've taken her to several more school dances, and I still don't feel young when I leave.

I admit I still have a long way to go when it comes to appreciating Jessie's taste in music, but I'm making progress. Justin Bieber's song *U Smile* is about young romance, but I've mentally revised it for a father-daughter relationship. When she plays it, I sing along. I might be loud and off-key, but that's okay, because when Jessie smiles, I smile.

I'm still hoping Jessie will help me find the fountain of youth. It wasn't at the end of the autograph line for Disney princesses and it sure hasn't been at her school dances. Maybe it will be on the tennis court — she just started lessons. I might not be youthful yet, but I'm staying optimistic.

Operation Slow-Down

"There is no way that my daughter is seven years old!" I look in the bathroom mirror. Scenes flash from the past – changing the thousandth dirty diaper, bathing my baby in the sink, pushing the stroller for the entire world to see the most beautiful girl, flying a spoon filled with delicious baby food in front of her face ... "Seven *months* old, not seven years!" I take a closer look in the bathroom mirror. I see added wrinkles, more gray, and a longer exposed forehead – more than seven months. Jessie is seven – it's true. Unfortunately, the wrinkles and hair changes, in both color and quantity, are true, too.

The Friday before the Georgia Southern students moved back in for the fall 2011 semester, I stopped at Daylight Donuts for breakfast. Glazed donuts are one of my weaknesses. Customers were lined up to the door. Having just begun writing my monthly MoMENts column, I decided to cherish the moment and wait patiently. Plus, I really wanted my glazed donuts. I noticed four young men sitting at one of the tables. Two of them were wearing "Operation Move-In" T-shirts. Operation Move-In volunteers help students move into their dorm rooms.

Next, my eyes were drawn to a little girl, about two years old, who was holding her baby doll. It brought a smile to my face, as that was just Jessie. A dad and his college-aged daughter were a few customers ahead in line.

My smile vanished. The way life is speeding by, that will soon be Jessie and me. The glazed donuts turned into comfort food.

Later that morning, I went to Walmart. Let's just say a person has plenty of time to soak up the moments at Walmart during the weekend the students return. I saw lots of parents with their college kids. One mom was taking a picture of her son in the check-out line with his purchases. That mom knew how to capture a memorable event in her son's life.

It seems like I just took the training wheels off of Jessie's bike. Then she was a kindergarten graduate. Now she is a big first grader. STOP! I'm declaring "Operation Slow-Down."

I'm not ready for Jessie's future years – training bras, makeup, braces, driver's education, or dating boys. Something tells me I'll never be ready for her to date boys. I'd like for the wrinkles, graying, and receding hairline to slow down, too. For now, I'm doing my best to enjoy each moment – from putting money under Jessie's pillow for lost teeth, to holding her hand while she's still happy to do it. And, when the time comes for Mattie and me to take her to college, I'm sure I'll be in the store line videoing and Mattie will be taking pictures.

For now, I need a donut.

Summer Camp Fun

Where did the school year go? I was just walking Jessie into her second-grade classroom for her first day of school. Of course, I had my camera and camcorder. I'm always carrying one or the other, or both, to capture memories of her firsts. She probably won't like it when I'm snapping pictures of her first date – come to think of it, I probably won't either. Mattie might need to snap that one. For now, I'm looking ahead to summer.

Somehow, the school year zoomed by and summer vacation is here. Jessie's summers have been enriched by all kinds of camps over her early years. Of course, these have not been the kind of camps where older children go to spend a week or more away from their parents. Mattie and I couldn't handle that yet. Instead, they are three-hour sessions over four or five consecutive days during the summer. There's been Kindermusik Camp, Kindergarten Camp, Cheer Camp for Girls, Fancy Nancy Camp, Reading Adventure Camp, Math Camp, Math and Science Camp, Soccer Camp, and Basketball Camp. Wow, I wish I had been able to plug into these camps as a boy. Okay, not Cheer Camp for Girls or Fancy Nancy Camp. Her summers also include Vacation Bible School and a trip to visit our out-of-state family and friends.

Not only do we have lots of pictures and video footage to capture this summer fun, we also have a box or two of the creations that Jessie makes during these

61

experiences. Whereas Mattie finds it difficult to clean out Jessie's closet and get rid of the cute clothes that she's outgrown, I have trouble throwing away my daughter's handiwork. One day when Jessie is older or we are out of storage room, we will look through the boxes of her masterful artwork and remember the fun times she had making them.

Although Jessie loves to attend camps with her friends, I hold fond memories of summer camps held right here at home. Water Camp involved squirt gun battles and watching Jessie run through the sprinklers in her bathing suit. Hey, the lawn needs watering and the girl needs a bath, so why not multi-task? It's amazing, too, how one little girl can get so drenched while helping her dad wash the family vehicles. I've learned there are major advantages to maintaining control of the hose, but sometimes she takes over and I end up soaked, instead of mildly saturated.

I've found Picnic Camp can be held in a variety of settings as long as snacks are involved. We've held picnic camps on the garage floor, in the back of the family van with all the seats and windows down, and in the bed of our pickup truck. A few coloring books, a box of crayons, paper, a few good books, and the CD player provide lots of entertainment.

We've also had numerous Learning Camps inside Jessie's tent set. This is not always the easiest setting for a 6'5" man to squeeze into, but I wouldn't miss it. It's amazing how much more fun math and writing are inside a tent instead of at the table. I've found that the blood always flows back into my legs within a few minutes of crawling back out. Unfortunately, I haven't been able to convince Jessie that Nap Camp would be awesome.

I'm not even going to tell our new puppy, Sadie, all the fun that's in store for her this summer. I know Dress-up Camp for dogs is already scheduled. As Sadie has previously modeled in several fashion shows and posed in all sorts of buckets, boxes, and bags, it seems kinder not to let her know what she's in for. Sadie will probably be glad when Jessie goes to some of her other camps.

In a blink of an eye, summer will be over and I'll be holding Jessie's hand as I walk my third grader to her classroom. And, who knows, when I get home after dropping Jessie off, I might just attend Nap Camp. I have a sneaking suspicion that Sadie will join me.

Holding On

So this is what it's going to feel like. I'm standing inside the screened porch looking at Jessie and a young man as they walk toward a lake for a fun date. My 7-year-old girl is wearing her life jacket with a whistle attached. She looks so grown up next to my wife's brother, Gary. For the past two days, he has taken Jessie out on the lake to teach her how to paddle a kayak.

It's great that Jessie has her mom and Uncle Gary to assist her with water sports as I don't swim well and am not comfortable around water. For the past two days, I've stood on the dock and taken lots of pictures and video footage of their kayak rides together. Today, however, Gary has a different plan. He's going to stand on the bank's edge and watch Jessie kayak across the lake and back, all by herself.

"She needs to build confidence," he said. He promised that if she gets in trouble, he would quickly get into his kayak and assist her. I'm not the least bit excited about this plan and want Gary to stay within a few feet of her at all times.

Don't get me wrong, I realize the importance of teaching children to be independent, cutting the apron strings, etc. – but not at age seven. I decided to stay on Gary's porch rather than watch. He assured me that with the water level down in the lake, Jessie could stand up at just about every spot and there's no danger of her being hit by a motorboat. She's wearing a life vest and has had lots of swimming lessons. I know she is safe, but still, I'm nervous.

They were only gone a few minutes when I had to look, even though I told myself I wouldn't. Jessie was about 50 yards out. I joined Gary and Mattie at the lake's edge. If Jessie got into trouble, I could run in and save my baby. Jessie reached the other end of the lake. I held my breath as she safely made her turn to come back. With about 50 yards to go, I could barely control myself. I cheered louder than Mattie and Gary combined. She did it!

What a great experience for Jessie. She learned a new skill. She learned to be independent in yet another area. She also learned if you set a goal and work toward it, you can achieve it.

I learned a couple of things, too. I need to shelter Jessie less. It's important for her to have life experiences that help her branch out and grow. I also learned that when a boy comes to the door to take my daughter out on her first date, I will feel like running after the car as it leaves the driveway. Fortunately, I have many, many years to come up with a plan for that, but I think an arrangement similar to the kayak situation might work okay. We could attach a whistle to Jessie's clothing and her mom, Uncle Gary, and I would watch the date closely and jump in to assist if we noticed any sign of trouble or heard the whistle.

For now the plan is simple – maximize our family experiences before another school year begins and scheduled activities take up so much of our time. For example, we're taking long bike rides together, which Jessie likes to lead. She used to follow. What happened?

In a few weeks, I plan to hold Jessie's hand as I walk her to her classroom for the first day of school. I know this morning routine will end before I'm ready. So I plan to stay in the moment and cherish life as a dad to a third grader. I'll cheer Jessie on as she masters her multiplication tables. We'll high five after she completes challenging assignments. I'll remind her it's "i" before "e" except after "c" as she prepares for her weekly spelling test. But, just as there are exceptions to this spelling rule, I realize parenting decisions won't always be clear-cut. My opinions will occasionally differ from Mattie's, like whether to allow Jessie to kayak solo across the lake. Together, we'll strive to find the right balance between allowing her to grow into an independent young woman and keeping her close and safe. For now, though, I'm holding on to summer. Too soon it will be time to let go.

Passes

Jessie and I are standing in line outside Peter Pan's Flight, a popular ride at Disney's Magic Kingdom. Luckily, we are in the FastPass line, which allows us to get into the shade and take flight much quicker than the visitors in the Stand-By line. As I ponder the joys of the FastPass, I wonder, wouldn't it be great if parents could reach into their wallets and pull out a pass to make every situation easier?

I could have used a Fast-Pass numerous times since Jessie's birth. I would have used one to speed up the process when Mattie and I were potty-training her. When Jessie whined and refused to bite anything for days because she wanted to keep her front baby tooth *forever*, a Fast-Pass would have enabled us to skip the crying and give it one quick yank. The Fast-Pass would be ideal to get Jessie to bed quickly, though she'd always choose the slower Stand-By line.

I can also think of other useful kinds of passes. I'd love to have a Redo-Pass for all the times I do stupid things, or that 20-20 hindsight suggests was not the best idea. Some are minor do-overs, like the time I stuck my finger into Jessie's diaper to determine if she had done a "number 2." I'd have needed another pass when I was a few seconds late getting a clean diaper onto Jessie. More important, I'd like to have a Redo-Pass for the times I lose patience and could better handle the responsibilities of parenthood.

Then there's the Take-A-Pass, which I'm confident I'd abuse. I'd use this pass to skip out on making supper when I'm tired. The Take-A-Pass could also be used when my creative 8-year-old wants me to play games where she invents the rules on the fly. In addition, I can only dress Barbie, brush her hair, and add accessories for so long before I'm ready to Take-A-Pass.

I guess I could pull out a Sleep-Pass instead. On second thought, I better save those for times of great exhaustion when I lose focus and do things like eat Jessie's Flintstones vitamins (pretty tasty) instead of mine, mix Jessie's oatmeal but forget to microwave it before serving, or make a pot of tea without the teabags.

If I could choose only one kind of pass, though, it would be the Slow-Pass. Jessie is growing up so quickly. As we stood in one of the lines at Disney, I noticed the top of her head already reaches Mattie's nose. I don't know how Jessie could be a third grader when I just took her to Pre-K last week. I'd also use a Slow-Pass when Jessie and I share desserts; I like toppings, too.

I'd definitely hand her a Slow-Pass before getting on the Teacups ride as excessive spinning turns me white. If I ever throw up on the Teacups, I'll need a Manly-Man-Pass to regain my pride, but that's a different story.

Most important, I'd use many Slow-Passes for Jessie to take her time when it comes to future decisions like selecting friends, choosing a college and career, and moving away. I'll need a Fast-Pass for exceeding the speed limit while going to visit her if she moves very far.

Parents face both joyous and frustrating times in rearing their children. Like lines at Disney, some move quickly and others not fast enough. Unfortunately, we can't whip out a Slow-Pass to make happy times last longer or a Fast-Pass to speed us through challenging situations. Instead, we do our best to read the signs and try to choose the right places to stand for the time and circumstances.

Today, Jessie proudly earned her Mickey Mouse Official Speedway License as she drove a racecar around the track with Mattie as her passenger. Mattie reported, "Her driving was terrible. She veered all over the place."

In another eight years or so, when Jessie wants to get her real driver's license, the Take-A-Pass will seem like a good option. However, I'll likely choose the Slow-Pass as I sit beside my teenage daughter, encouraging her to drive a few miles slower than the speed limit.

In the meantime, I'm placing a large order for Sleep-Passes. I have a feeling I'm going to need a big supply.

I Will

What will I do with my limited time? Finding the right balance is a constant struggle.

This summer, 8-year-old Jessie and I traveled to Pennsylvania for our annual visit with family and friends. I can't remember another two-day trip with so much rain. The hour-long traffic jam didn't add to the fun. I also could have done without the brisk walk down six flights of stairs at 4:25 a.m. when the fire alarm went off in our hotel. At least it was a mechanical problem and not a fire. By the time I reached the Mason-Dixon Line, I was ready for a little "me" time.

While Jessie fished with her granddaddy, I drove to the cemetery to pay my respects to a few loved ones. I agree the cemetery is not the most exciting place for "me" time, but as I visited each grave, many wonderful memories surfaced – along with a few tears.

My next stop was the ball field where I spent much of my childhood. I stepped into the batter's box, tapped my imaginary bat at the corner of the plate like I'd done hundreds of times with a real one, and swung at a few make-believe pitches. The memory of the grand-slam home run I hit 40 years ago came flooding back.

I walked around the bases. I could have run, but I wanted to soak up the memories. As I rounded second base, I put on my pretend glove and fielded a few grounders at the shortstop position. I was a boy again and it felt good.

When I got back to the house, Jessie excitedly reported she caught her first fish, a 14-inch bass according to Granddaddy, though Jessie told me it was 2-feet long when stretched out. The fish, having been returned to the pond, couldn't clarify the matter.

Though the time alone had rejuvenated me, I was disappointed to have missed seeing her bass, no matter its size. "Me" time is important, but family time is better.

Now, not seeing Jessie's first fish is one thing, but missing her wedding? Recently, I ran an errand and when I returned, Jessie greeted me wearing her mother's wedding dress.

"I was only gone 20 minutes!" I exclaimed. She and Mattie had cleaned out a closet while I was gone. Mattie's wedding gown was too big for Jessie, but not by much. Seeing her took me back to my wedding day 28 years ago and the vow I made when asked if I would love, honor, and cherish my bride. I will.

As another fast year comes to a close, I'm thinking about how I will spend my time in the new year. I will continue to keep the promise I made to love, honor, and cherish my wife. I will put gas in Mattie's car because she rarely looks at her gas gauge. I will come running when I hear, "Spider!" I will take the dog out when it's early, late, cold, or rainy. I will make sure our bathrooms never run out of toilet tissue. And, as often as possible, I will hand

Mattie a glass of iced tea as soon as she wakes up, and let her keep my favorite pillow when she falls asleep first.

I will also enjoy some "me" time to play tennis and pursue my writing goals. I will nurture relationships with phone calls, letters, and visits, and will remember loved ones no longer with us. Most important, I will spend quality time with Jessie. I will shoot baskets, watch her improvised shows, and eat her beautifully decorated cupcakes after showing proper appreciation for her artistic talent.

One day, Jessie may be dressed in a wedding gown for real, and as with the 4:25 a.m. hotel fire alarm, I won't be ready. In the meantime, I will cherish my time with her. Soon, I will hang her Christmas stocking and enjoy filling it with little girl things.

Each day, I will step up to the plate – not at the ball field, but as a father – looking out for her well-being. And, when I throw balls onto the roof of our house and Jessie catches them in her pink glove on the bounce off the driveway, I will remember that fatherhood is even better than a grand-slam home run. In a few years I will have plenty of "me" time, some of which I will spend missing these hectic days with my daughter.

Quite a Ride

Parenting can be quite a ride, and I'm not referring to the spinning Tea Cups at Disney or sailboat rides with Jessie's Uncle Gary. Some rides, you don't want to get off.

"Hey, that was my daughter who just made that 12-foot basket!"

"Jessie, this is an excellent report card!"

"You look so beautiful in your Easter dress, Jessie!" Other rides don't end quickly enough, such as birthday parties with screaming kids sugared up on cake and ice cream. For still other rides, I wonder, "Why did I get on?" I'm thinking of the time 3-year-old Jessie pulled my shorts down on an elevator, exposing my jock strap to the other passengers.

Recently, I took Jessie, age nine, on a daddy-daughter date to our church's annual festival. Having made a few mistakes in the past, I try my best not to say anything that might embarrass Jessie in front of her friends. I still haven't mastered this discipline, even though my comments are always out of love and concern. I guess it could be worse. One mom told me her daughter made her sign a "Do Not Embarrass Me" contract.

As soon as we arrived at the festival, Jessie's "find friends" antennae went up. She climbed up and slid down a tall inflatable slide, with eyes peeled for friends. She did close her eyes when she had her hair spray-painted orange, blue, and green. Of course, I had my camera. Parents can't have too many photos of their children.

Then Jessie spied Alice, and I dutifully found an inconspicuous place to stand as I watched the girls play. Okay, I did take pictures of Jessie and Alice at the cakewalk, but only a few.

The three of us ate hot dogs and burgers together before heading to one of my favorite parts of the festival – the hayride. As we were preparing to climb on, Jessie turned around and said, "Dad, may I take the ride with just Alice?" This caught me completely off guard. I maintained a stiff upper lip and brokenheartedly gave my approval. This "letting go" stuff isn't easy. I can't say I'm very good at it either.

After I took a few pictures of the girls sitting on a bale of hay at the rear of the ungated wagon, I said, "Alice, you keep an eye on Jessie." Dang, the second I finished the sentence, I knew I had embarrassed Jessie … and her nonverbal communication confirmed it. I quickly came back with, "Jessie, you watch after Alice, too." Good save, Daddy.

While the girls enjoyed their hayride, I commiserated with the parents of a 12-year-old daughter. She was off enjoying the festival with a friend, too.

As the festival came to a close, Jessie and I were headed to the parking lot when we saw the wagon loading for one final trip. We ran to get on. Jessie called, "first," then promptly sat on the first bale as she stepped onto the wagon. I was a happy "second" as I took the seat next to the pretty girl with orange, blue, and green hair. I cherished the moment with my arm curled around my daughter to keep her safe during the ride.

I wish I could end the story here with the wagon riding out into the night with its passengers living happily ever after. However, back in the car, on what should have been a blissful drive home, Jessie shocked me with another request. From the backseat, she asked, "Dad, can you just drop me off at the festival next year and let me play with my friends? You can talk with the other parents." Thank goodness the steering wheel caught my chin.

I don't know what lies ahead in my parenting world. I wish it would be as easy as calling "second," to be with Jessie for important events. Yet, I know the time will come when I'll be lucky to make the top five. Whatever my spot, I'm looking forward to sharing lots of good rides, maybe just not as many as I thought. At least I'll get to talk with other parents. It helps to know I'm not alone.

The Right Number

It's hard to believe I'll be celebrating my 11th Father's Day as a dad this year. My baby girl, now 10, stands 5 feet tall. It doesn't seem possible, but the numbers don't lie.

We live in a world filled with numbers – dates, times, measurements, bank accounts, thermostat settings, weights, ages, house numbers, bills, paychecks, ball scores, and many more.

Of course, some numbers are more important than others. I prefer Jessie's grades to be in the 90s or 100. Being a college football fan, I hope my teams score more points than their opponents each Saturday. I don't count the number of hairs on my head, but I'd rather have a bigger number. It doesn't take an auditor to know that some of them have gone missing in recent years.

Sunday afternoon, Jessie provided Mattie and me with an interesting numbers challenge. About two weeks earlier, Mattie had a business trip. Rather than leave her home office unused while she was gone, I set up Jessie's tent and tunnels. Long ago, my tall girl outgrew the tent, a gift for her second birthday, but she still loves to play in it. The square tent measures just 4 feet long by 4 feet wide. It is 42 inches tall at the highest point, and connects to one of the four tunnels that came with the set. Jessie had a blast playing with Sadie in the tent and tunnels.

She even slept in the tent during Mattie's absence. Well, part of her slept in the tent. About half of the sleeping bag containing Jessie's legs stretched outside the opening. The small tent held quite a bit – a girl, a dog, 14 stuffed animals, one pet pillow, three small pillows, three regular pillows, and several blankets for padding. Each night, I'd place a battery-operated lantern in one of the tunnels, which made a great night-light.

When Mattie came home from her trip, Jessie asked to have one final party in the tent before we took it down. She planned the entire event from food to attire, so all her mom and I had to do was show up. Jessie handed me one of her headbands to wear, while Mattie lucked out with a tiara. Sadie looked cute in the feather boa Jessie wrapped around her neck. The people menu consisted of peanut butter cookies and Kool-Aid. Sadie's plate held a spoonful of peanut butter, Rice Krispies, and a few pieces of leftover chicken.

Now, here is where the numbers problem began. Jessie not only invited Mattie, Sadie, and me to the party, but also 14 stuffed animals. When Jessie throws a party, she throws a party!

I've heard about cramming people into things, such as a Volkswagen, phone booth, photo booth, even an outhouse. Mattie, Sadie, Jessie, 14 stuffed animals, and I were about to take the "tent stuffing" challenge. At 6'5", I knew I would take up my fair share of the space. With the 14 animals already arranged, Queen Mattie and

Showgirl Sadie went in next. Jessie and I squeezed in last, with our cookie plates and Sadie's snacks. We opted to leave the drinks outside the tent (smart thinking by Dad).

"Dad, don't sit on Eeyore!" Luckily, I didn't sit on Sadie's spoonful of peanut butter.

We all made it in, but after getting kicked, twice, within the first minute; I opted to enjoy my cookies and Kool-Aid from the outside looking in. I like it when blood flows to all my extremities, while not being chided for smashing a donkey. Prior to the conclusion of the party, we all crammed into the tent a second time for a "famie" photo (a selfie of our family).

Each day, we're surrounded by numbers – some within our control, others not. Sometimes we're happy when the number is big, like a bonus in our paycheck. Other times, such as when looking down at the bathroom scale, small numbers are better. Some numbers speed by too quickly, like Jessie's age, a number that will end in teen before I know it. Is there such a thing as "the perfect number?" For a few minutes on a Sunday afternoon, we sure found a good one. I have a "famie" to prove it.

Fields of Dreams

The kick went up. The football sailed through the uprights. "It's good!"

What made this kick special? My fourth-grader Jessie and I had just witnessed the first field goal kicked by a female varsity football player in her school's history. I used the opportunity to make two important points to Jessie — "If you set a goal and work hard, you can achieve it" and "follow your dreams."

I must admit, though, to having told friends and family members, "I'm glad I have a girl because football is such a rough sport." It hadn't occurred to me that my daughter might play football. I'd worry every second Jessie played, even if she had pads on her shoulders and a mouthpiece to protect her teeth. Lucky for me, at least so far, Jessie hasn't expressed interest in football, except for cheering on her favorite high school and college teams with Dad by her side.

Speed ahead a few weeks. Our field goal kicker began the game by kicking off to the opposing team. Their player caught the ball, took a few steps left and then reversed course. He found a seam, and down the field he ran to what looked like a sure touchdown. But at the 30-yard line, our field goal kicker tackled him. The home crowd's exuberance over the tackle was short-lived, though, as a few seconds later, she limped off the field with a leg injury.

The trainer looked at our kicker's left knee as she stretched her leg out on the sideline. The kicker stood up and walked gingerly, bending over several times to inspect her knee. She didn't return to the action.

As the game continued, I noticed a man, I'm confident the girl's father, walk up to her on the sideline. Though I couldn't hear the conversation, my guess is it went something like this.

"Hi, kiddo. How are you doing?"

"Dad, I injured my left knee. It really hurts."

"We'll get it checked out and go from there. Hang tough. For tonight, support your team from the sideline."

Before he walked away, I saw the dad bend over and tap his daughter's thigh pad with the back of his right hand. "By the way, nice tackle."

The dad appeared calm, and the tap was a touching gesture. If Jessie had been the one lying on the sideline, the scene probably would have played out more like this.

I jump from the aluminum bleachers and bump into the spectator sitting next to me, knocking his hot dog from its roll. I run across the track and accidentally take out the trainer as I speed to Jessie's side. "My baby! My baby!" I pick her up in my arms and race the 50 yards to where the ambulance is parked during each game, all the while screaming, "To the hospital!"

Okay, I don't think I'd make a good father to a football-playing daughter. Would I learn to adjust, like I've had to during all of Jessie's life stages? Probably so.

Obviously, I want Jessie to follow her dreams. She's a determined young lady, and will make her mark on this world in the fields of her choice. Would it be easier if her passions were in sync with those of her parents? Maybe, but so far it's looking like that's not the case. Her tennis racquet strings aren't worn nearly enough and she'd rather put outfits on our Shetland sheepdog than shoot baskets in the driveway. But Mattie and I will do our best to support Jessie's goals, whatever they are.

Like the ball kicked high at the start of this story, I know there'll be things going up in Jessie's future, like her hand in the classroom and her eyebrows when she gets excited. I'm impressed by how high she kicks her legs when she dances. Before I know it, she'll be lifting her tassel at her high school graduation. In the meantime, I'll enjoy each report card, dog fashion show, and dance recital. Above all, Jessie will know her parents love her and are filled with pride when she excels at whatever she decides to do, whether she makes a touchdown-saving tackle or hoists a tennis trophy. I'm pulling for the latter – in doubles – with me as her partner. Hey, a dad can dream, too.

Chapter 4

MoMENts of Sighs and Surprise

Energy – There's a 44-year difference between the dates on Jessie's birth certificate and mine. According to Jessie, I'm the second-oldest father in her fourth-grade class. Thank goodness tennis has kept me in good shape, because children need parents who possess lots of energy.

According to the *law of conservation of energy*, energy cannot be created or destroyed, only transferred from one object to another, or transformed from one form to another. Sometimes it feels like all of my energy is transferring to Jessie, as she has plenty and I'm always running low. This basic law of physics will be my friend when I figure out how Jessie can transfer some of her ample energy to me.

Cherish the Moments

"What's the purpose of living in the world if we don't cherish the moments?" My 7-year-old Jessie said this yesterday evening. She is wise beyond her years. Not to mention, she reads my column.

Yesterday was a busy day. In the morning I finished proofreading a manuscript I'd been working on for months, then emailed it to a literary agent. After lunch, I mowed, trimmed, and edged for about two hours in the hot sun with temperatures in the 90s. After a quick shower, I picked up Jessie from school. I was able to squeeze in a 15-minute power nap while Jessie watched a little TV. She likes to watch *Let's Make a Deal* when she gets home. Maybe that's how she's gotten so good at negotiating – she's always trying to make a deal. I did a load of laundry and boiled eggs. While Jessie did her homework, I worked on paperwork.

Mattie called to say she would be home late. I prepared supper. Jessie *helped*. She loves to *help*. Since she reads my stories, I won't elaborate, but I trust that readers will get my point. After supper, I asked Jessie if she wanted to help dry dishes and she quickly jumped at the opportunity. She noticed the newly purchased lantern sitting in the kitchen. Mattie had brought it home a week earlier, and I had just put batteries in it the night before.

Jessie had an idea, "Let's do dishes by lantern light!" Being already tired, I was not up for the plan. Before the word "No" could come out of my mouth, though, Jessie had the lantern by the sink and the kitchen lights turned out. A brief discussion ensued during which she made her points as quickly as possible without taking a breath so that I couldn't get an opening to say no. I was ready to end the discussion when she said, "What's the purpose of living in the world if we don't cherish the moments?"

Over the next hour, Jessie and I washed and dried dishes, read a book, and did *Brain Quest* cards by the light of a battery-operated lantern. Jessie pointed out how much electricity we were saving in addition to all of the fun we were having. Mattie came home after 7:30. I lay sprawled out on the sofa holding the lantern while Jessie ran to the door to welcome her momma home. She excitedly shouted, "Daddy and I are cherishing the moments!" Mattie walked into the dimly lit living room, took one look at me, and could tell for sure that's what we had been doing.

Jessie keeps a daily journal in which she records the highlight of each day. The lantern-lit activities topped her list yesterday. They topped mine, too. I came very close to not letting her use the lantern, but I'm so glad I did. It turned ordinary chores into fun time spent together. In some ways it was a little thing, but it turned out to be the "Big Deal of the Day" for Jessie.

Call Me, Maybe

"Call Me Maybe." This Carly Rae Jepsen song is currently at the top of Jessie's favorite songs list. It's about a girl who wants a boy to call her. After hearing Jessie sing it so many times, the song has grown on me. Jessie's got my number – 1-800-NEED-DAD. She calls me, not maybe, but definitely and often.

It's amazing how each school day at 7 a.m., I have to call Jessie two or more times, turn on the lights, or bring her orange juice so she can take a few sips to help wake up. I can't imagine what it would take to get her moving if she didn't like school. However, when the family can sleep in on weekends, early in the morning I can expect Jessie's call, "Daddy, I'm awake!" Call me? Maybe she could call Momma instead?

I've come to realize that "Daddy" can be called too many times. "Daddy – spider!" "Daddy, I'm out of toilet tissue." "Daddy, I need a bar of soap." And Jessie's favorite, "Daddy, watch me." I hate to say this, but there is some possibility my beloved only child is a tiny bit spoiled. Mattie and I are trying to teach Jessie to be more independent, but Mattie finds it easier than I do to give her the busy signal when Jessie calls for things she could do for herself or when she just wants attention. That's probably why Jessie never calls "Momma, I'm awake."

On a recent car trip, I noticed a billboard that read, "Call your parents." It spoke to me both as a son and a father, and I kept thinking about it during the long drive home.

I imagine that many parents of adult children sometimes wish, like the girl in Jepsen's song, that their kids would call. I'm blessed I can still call my mother. Since I've become a stay-at-home dad, I've called her numerous times to say "Thank you for all you did for me" and "You raised four of these!" So often I wish I could call my dad, who passed away in 2009. I also call family members, mine and Mattie's, and a few dear friends to seek advice or share the ups and downs of life.

As a father, I'm on-duty for "Daddy" calls 24/7. Parents can't record a message that says, "No one is available to take your call. Please leave a message or call back between 9 a.m. and 5 p.m., Monday through Friday." Occasionally, we may "transfer the call" to the other spouse or grandparents.

As a new year begins, I'm going to enjoy as many "Watch me, Daddy!" calls as I can, even when they come in earlier than I'd like. Mattie and I realize that too soon the calls will come less frequently. Perhaps in the future, Jessie will call Mattie and me to thank us for all we did for her and to seek our advice. In the meantime, I'm going to make frequent calls to my mother and do my best to maintain spider-free living conditions for Jessie.

Embarrassing Love

As I drove Jessie to school last Friday, I quizzed her on multiplication tables in preparation for the day's math test. She answered accurately except for one problem, 8 x 4. I had her repeat it three times in the car to reinforce the answer. As we were walking into the school, one of Jessie's friends came running up. I followed the two girls to their classroom. I might as well have gone back to my car as I became invisible to them, even though I was only a step behind.

As they neared the entrance to their classroom, I said, "Have a good day, girls." That line didn't draw a response. But then I said, "Remember, Jessie, 8 x 4 = 32." Jessie turned around quickly. "Dad!" Jessie's verbal and nonverbal communication made it clear that I had embarrassed her in front of her friend.

It wasn't my first mistake as a parent and it surely won't be the last. I only wanted her to score a good grade on her test, but I guess I was guilty of "embarrassing love." As I drove home, I recalled how my parents had embarrassed me with their love 30 years earlier.

I was in my early 20s and still lived with them in Pennsylvania. I had driven over to visit Mattie, my girlfriend at the time, who lived about five miles away. It was snowing, so I parked my car at the top of her farm lane and walked down the half-mile gravel road to her house. If I had driven down the lane, I wouldn't have been able to get my 1967 Buick Special back up the hill to go home. When you're in love, walking a mile (round trip) in freezing temperatures is nothing.

Mattie's family and I were inside their house playing ping pong and having a good time when we heard a vehicle drive down the lane and stop in front of the barn. Mattie's brother looked out the window and announced, "It's Pat's mom and dad." Sure enough, my dad was at the wheel of his four-wheel-drive International Scout and Mom peered out the window from the seat next to him.

I walked out and asked my parents why they were there. They said that with the freezing weather and more snow in the forecast, they wanted to make sure I made it home safely. Maybe it's a "man" thing, but when you're in your early 20s, your *mommy and daddy* don't come to your date's house to take you home. I was mortified and furious, but I returned to the house, calmly said goodbye to Mattie and her family, and climbed into the Scout.

I said a lot as we drove up the half-mile hill to pick up my car. I said more when we got home, and the discussion continued the following morning. I wanted to make sure they never embarrassed me like that again. Looking back, I know my parents acted out of love and concern. Was I embarrassed? For sure. Did my male ego take a hit? Definitely! Did it make a difference in the whole scheme of things? No. I made it home safely and forgave my parents. Mattie kept dating me and became my bride a few years later.

Now that I'm a father myself, I understand parents' first instincts are to help and protect their children. We only want what's best, or what we think is best, for our kids. Going forward, I'll do my best not to embarrass Jessie. I'm doing better already. This morning over breakfast, I reminded her to punctuate her sentences when she takes her spelling test. My quizzes will stop, however, when I pull the car into her school parking lot. And when Jessie becomes a teenager and goes on a date to the movies, you won't see me walking into the theatre should she forget her sweater. I'll have Mattie take it in while I wait in the parking lot.

Oh, by the way, Jessie aced her math test.

Twists and Turns

"No high-impact activities." These were four words I didn't want to hear from my orthopedist. He ordered an MRI on my sore right knee and sent me home, still hobbling. How was I going to cope without tennis?

When I arrived home, I explained to Mattie I wouldn't be able to do housework anymore, but she didn't agree with my classification of vacuuming as a high-impact activity. Jessie didn't cut me any breaks, either. She soon set up an obstacle course that required jumping rope, shooting a basketball, and kicking a soccer ball. She cut me some slack by leaving out the hula-hoop. Unable to turn down her challenge, I tentatively worked my way through the obstacles in just under two minutes. Jessie won by 55 seconds.

Life is full of twists and turns. One minute you're on the tennis court attacking the net with the catlike swiftness of a 20-year-old. The next, you're limping with an inflamed, throbbing knee, making your mark in the *Guinness Book of World Records* for the slowest time to cover a 10-yard stretch from the bed to the toilet.

A few days after my humbling obstacle-course defeat, I met with the orthopedist to review my MRI results. "A large tear of the medial meniscus," he said. This certainly sounded severe enough to get me out of vacuuming. Maybe even grocery shopping, laundry, and washing dishes, too. My doctor suggested that a 30-45 minute operation, followed by six weeks of recovery with no high-impact activities, was the best way to get me back on the courts.

Being someone who likes to make well-informed decisions, I Googled *medial meniscus*. I found a source that said if the patient would stay in bed for six weeks, the meniscus would probably heal.

Jessie thought this was a great idea. "Momma and I will take care of you," she said. "You can check my homework in bed and I can bring your computer so you can work in bed." I told Jessie that although this sounded pretty good, I couldn't stay in bed for six weeks.

Undeterred, she devised two different ways for me to walk that eliminated the need to bend my knees. Both waddle-like techniques were better suited for a penguin. Nevertheless, I was touched by Jessie's compassion and her willingness to take care of me.

Then I happened to mention that if I decided to have the operation, I'd have to use crutches for three days. Her eyes lit up. "Yay! I get to use your crutches!" She ran into the kitchen and pulled two chairs back to back. She threw her arms over the chair backs with her armpits resting on the tops, smiling ear-to-ear as she attempted to use the chairs like crutches. So much for compassion.

Don Williams, Jr., an American novelist and poet, said, "The road of life twists and turns and no two directions are ever the same. Yet our lessons come from the journey, not the destination." Who knows what journeys are ahead? I'm afraid my best days of winning tennis trophies might be behind me – unless Jessie becomes my mixed doubles partner and has enough game to carry me. It's also likely I'll lose a few more obstacle-course challenges and will never be the family hula-hoop champion. However, I plan to enjoy my journey through whatever high- or low-impact activities come my way, even vacuuming.

Parents do lots of low-impact activities that have a big impact. They hug, kiss, laugh, feed, bandage, encourage, celebrate, listen, and pray. Fortunately, I can do these activities forever, regardless of my age or the condition of my knees. And someday, if Jessie asks to walk with my crutches, I'll try to convince her to walk behind the vacuum cleaner instead.

Windows and Wheels

Why did I have to see *that* when I peered out from my in-laws' patio on Christmas morning? It could have been anything, a rambunctious squirrel, a trespassing dog, or low-flying vultures. Instead, I saw a teenage girl run across my in-laws' backyard to the rear window of her house. She paused at the window and looked toward the street. She blew two kisses to, I'm guessing, the friend who dropped her off. Then she carefully lifted the window from the outside, crawled into her house, and closed the window and blinds behind her.

As a parent, I had trouble swallowing what I had just witnessed. If my daughter was sneaking out of the house for who knows what kind of get together, I'd want to know about it. I'd certainly rather deal with it now than nine months later when there could be additional issues. However, I didn't know the people, and wouldn't want to cause trouble between my in-laws and their new neighbors. I decided to mind my own business; yet, I couldn't get it out of my head.

About an hour later, I was helping Jessie with her new purple dress. As I buttoned it up in the back and tied the bow around her waist, I flashed back to the teenage girl I had seen earlier that morning. It feels like I was just changing Jessie's diaper. Now she's eight years old, wearing size 10 dresses, and stands as tall as her mother's chin.

I felt it was time for a talk. No, not "the talk" as Mattie will cover that one. This one I could handle. I told Jessie she must never sneak out of the house. Her response didn't put me completely at ease, though I accepted it. She said "I'll check with Momma." Maybe she knows that Dad will say no more quickly when it comes to dating decisions.

Later on Christmas Day, Jessie opened a special gift – a pair of roller skates. The next day, we went to the park to break them in. Mattie stood on one side holding her hand while I provided a steady force on the other side. Even though Jessie had on her helmet and elbow- and knee-pads, I still worried. We went back to the park to practice again on the following two days. Jessie improved dramatically each day. On the third day, Mattie just watched while I held my daughter's hand.

Then Jessie said it. "Daddy, you need to let go." Reluctantly, I released her hand but remained within catching distance behind her. Uncle Gary laughed at me as I zoomed in ready for the catch each time Jessie flailed her arms. His laughter didn't bother me, though, because I was right where I needed to be.

Later, I again thought about the teenage girl in the window, knowing Jessie's teenage years aren't far away. I realize more "letting go" times are ahead. I also know it's not possible to catch all the falls. I'm hoping that because I've stood beside Jessie when she learns to skate, and for many of the other important times of her childhood, I'll never have to stand guard outside her bedroom window.

I've concluded that parenting requires seeing your child through a series of wheels – stroller, wagon, tricycle, training, bicycle, scooter, and now roller skates. I'm going to enjoy the pink-skate-wheels stage to the fullest. Something tells me seeing Jessie behind the wheel of a car will be much harder. When that time comes, I'll be beside her in the front seat. Then it will be time for Daddy to let go again, and Mattie and I will find ourselves peering out the window, waiting for her safe return home.

A Truckload of Kisses

Jessie loves to have picnics. I can't tell you how many we've shared in her young life. Our picnics can be held anywhere. We sometimes park the family van under the shade tree in our yard and open the sunroof and windows. On other occasions, I'll throw a blanket in the bed of my pickup truck or on the garage floor. For our dog, Sadie's first birthday, Jessie held a picnic party on her bedroom floor and invited several stuffed animals. Rice Krispies covered the just-vacuumed floor, and Jessie sat on the tiny cup of peanut butter she had made for Sadie, but Jessie had fun and Sadie appeared to have a happy birthday.

Jessie often asks, "Could we have a picnic?" so I wasn't surprised she requested one for our last lunch of 2013. With the weather cloudy and cool, I voted to eat at the kitchen table, but she really wanted to have a picnic outside. I vetoed throwing a blanket on the lawn and told her the garage floor was too cold. Mattie had the van at work. My "never give up" daughter suggested the bed of the pickup truck. We had washed it recently, so she knew I couldn't use the "it's dirty" excuse. So I made the logical choice; I surrendered. It's happened before and it will happen again.

Jessie said, "Don't look, please" about five times as she prepared the picnic for the three "D's" – dad, daughter, and dog. She likes to surprise me with the menu.

When she had everything ready, we took our picnic outside, which required a few trips. I threw an old blanket in the truck bed, and then retrieved Sadie, who attends every picnic. The temperature was in the low 50's and the breeze made it cool, but not like the winters where I grew up in Pennsylvania. Sadie promptly spilled her water all over the blanket. Jessie ripped off her shoes and socks, as all picnics require bare feet. She then carefully unwrapped the aluminum foil from the items she had packed. We had cheese, raisins, nuts, and crackers for dipping in the peanut butter and honey she had mixed. She also packed juice boxes, fruit cups, and granola bars. Jessie even remembered napkins and plastic utensils. Of course, we had dessert, too – a piece of chocolate candy for her, Oreo cookies for me. Okay, lunch may not have covered all the basic food groups, but we were having an enjoyable daddy-daughter picnic.

As we ate, I played one of my favorite songs, "Butterfly Kisses," on my phone. I was enjoying the lyrics when Jessie asked, "Do you know there are five different kinds of kisses?" I was afraid to ask, but did anyway. "What are the five kinds?" Jessie responded, "regular, butterfly, blown, Eskimo, and French." Luckily, I wasn't sitting near the edge of the open truck gate, lest I would have fallen out onto the concrete driveway. I bravely decided to ask a follow-up question. "What is a

French kiss?" Jessie responded, "The tongues touch when kissing."

Apparently, Mattie had covered this topic with her. For sure, I hadn't. I admire Mattie for always answering Jessie's questions. But how did we go from butterfly kisses to teenage topics? When the song ended, Jessie reached over and found Taylor Swift's "22" on my phone. She played it twice. I'm definitely not ready for Jessie to feel 22.

As I'm finishing this story, I'm hungry. My picnic lunch has worn off. In a few hours, the giant ball will drop over Times Square. Prior to midnight, I'll lean over my sleeping daughter and give her forehead a "regular" kiss before I go to bed. I'm glad she's 9, not 22, so I still have a few years to give her bedtime kisses. I'm sure the future holds many more picnics, too. Maybe I can convince her to pack me a sandwich next time. I also think we'll have more of our picnics in the yard. The grass makes for a softer landing.

I Hope You Twirl

I'm a fan of Lee Ann Womack's song, "I Hope You Dance," which beautifully expresses parents' desires for their children to live life to the fullest. When I think about my life, many of the times I most regret are not the things I did, but the times I did nothing. I wish I had gone out for my high school's basketball team. Maybe I would have been a bench warmer, but I also could have scored a winning basket or grabbed a key rebound. At minimum, I would have been a good teammate.

Though shy in school, I wish I'd mustered up enough nerve to ask a girl to my high school prom. In fact, there were a number of girls I wish I had asked out during my teenage years. What's the worst thing a girl could have said? "No." Well, I guess she could have laughed in my face. Or she might have whispered to all her friends sitting around the cafeteria, "Hey, you'll never guess what Patrick just asked me. Can you believe it?" Sure, their giggles would have hurt. However, the girl could also have said, "Yes, I'd love to go out with a tall, handsome, smart, sweet, sensitive, funny guy like you. I thought you'd never ask. All my girlfriends will be so jealous you asked me and not them." Okay, my guess is the girl's response likely would have fallen somewhere in between. However, I never asked and my shoes never scuffed the dance floor.

Jessie loves to dance. She takes ballet lessons once a week, but her dancing doesn't stop when she leaves the studio. She's twirling all the time, from the kitchen to the bathroom, from the living room to the bedroom, and even across the school parking lot. If there's space for a spin, my girl will be twirling (or doing a cartwheel). This is usually not a bad thing; the key word here is "usually."

One recent evening, my family was enjoying strawberry shortcake in the living room. Unfortunately, Jessie's shortcake and strawberries didn't come out even. She asked if she could have another small piece of shortcake. As she rushed to the kitchen holding her glass plate filled with strawberry juice, I said, "Don't run." A few seconds later, I heard the noise I wanted to avoid when I said, "Don't run."

By the time I made it to the kitchen, Jessie had already retrieved the dustpan and broom to begin cleanup. I assessed the damage. Pieces of broken glass had flown everywhere. Somehow, glass had even landed in the living room and dining room. As Jessie and I cleaned up, my sneakers sticking to the juice-covered floor with each step, I noticed strawberry juice on the side and front of the refrigerator. Red liquid dripped down the refrigerator from my shoulder level (not good since I'm 6'5"). The juice had splattered all over the kitchen countertop and speckled the items on it, a loaf of bread, a camera, my wallet, and a recently purchased music CD. I paused before looking up at the ceiling, afraid of what I might see. Thankfully, the ceiling remained strawberry-free.

I needed an explanation as I couldn't figure out how a single, dropped plate of strawberry juice could have covered half our house. Jessie sheepishly admitted that as she came into the kitchen, she did one, *only one*, twirl. Unfortunately, during her spin the glass plate smashed into the side of the refrigerator and, well, the rest is sugary-juice and broken-glass history.

As I painstakingly mopped the floor, worried I might miss a small shard of glass that could stick in someone's foot, I can't say I "cherished the moment." After a well-earned night of sleep, though, I thought, "Isn't it great that Jessie spins with happiness?"

One day, Jessie and I will talk about this story and laugh. In the meantime, Jessie, I hope you always twirl … just not when you're holding a juice-filled glass plate, or knives, or cartons of eggs (Sadie would probably appreciate it if you'd stop twirling with her, too). But I especially wish that your life overflows with wonderful experiences as you twirl through it.

Oh, one more piece of advice for when you're older. When a boy musters up enough courage to ask you out on a date, feel free to say "No," but do it nicely. Don't have a gigglefest with your girlfriends and hurt his feelings.

When Life Throws You Branches

Let's face it; life is filled with speed bumps, hurdles, hills, even a mountain or two. In this morning's mail, I received a jury summons. As I read the green paper, my shoulders slumped, followed by a mumbled "I don't have time to sit on a jury." Sitting nearby, Jessie witnessed her dad's verbal and nonverbal reaction. I try to maintain a positive attitude and set a good example for her when trials pop up (in this case literally and figuratively). For this particular incident, though, I wouldn't have wanted a judge to ask, "Has the jury reached a verdict on whether Patrick Hempfing responded to the situation in accordance with good-role-model standards?" A hung jury would have been my best chance.

A few weeks before the jury summons, a big storm came through and took down a huge part of the crabapple tree next to our driveway. My initial reaction was, "Ah, man. I don't have time for this mess." I knew the project would require lots of sawing and numerous trips to the dump in my pickup truck. Alternatively, it would have cost a couple of Ben Franklins to have a tree service come out to do the cleanup.

Jessie, looking at the same damage from the storm, had a different reaction. "Dad, we can build a tree fort!" I calmly informed Jessie I didn't see a tree fort in our future.

"But Dad, when is the next time we're going to have a chance for a tree fort? We can have parties in it." Of course, she batted her eyelashes to influence my decision. I've always had a weak spot for fluttering eyelashes, Mattie's or Jessie's.

Over the days that followed, I strategically sawed the bigger branches, while Jessie snipped the smaller ones. The largest snapped branch had not fallen to the ground, but propped against the tree, providing a teepee effect. Jessie and I cut a path into and out of our fort. Since we didn't have a civil engineer to evaluate the structural integrity, I sawed an "emergency exit" for Sadie. In the event the fort collapsed, Sadie could run out for help. I also cleared a little spot, like a beaver's lodge, where Jessie, Sadie, and I could sit with the leaves shading us from the sun. I was careful not to saw any "supporting beams."

As temperatures hovered around 90 degrees, sweat dripped from my nose and perspiration saturated every stitch of my clothing. Jessie made me laugh when she went inside our fort and said, "It feels like fall in here."

Instead of throwing cut branches into the back of my pickup, thereby expediting the clean-up project, I slung a few of them on top of one "wall" that needed to be higher according to my "supervising fort architect." Jessie and I lifted another big branch into place, but it caught other branches and they slung back and smacked me in the side of the face. At that point, I may not have selected the word "fun," a word Jessie kept repeating, to describe our project.

Five days and several trips to the dump later, we finished the "best tree fort ever." Jessie made a batch of Kool-Aid while I placed a chair and stool inside our "lodge." She brought a plateful of cookies we had baked earlier. As I drank my blue raspberry lemonade and snacked on delicious cookies, I reflected on the fort-building days. Jessie had seen the opportunity for a cherished moment, not hours of work under the hot Georgia sun. She had demonstrated the importance of a good attitude, which turned what could have been a big inconvenience into a wonderful daddy-daughter project, and one of the highlights of our summer. I also got lots of exercise, and the branches will soon be ground into mulch for someone's garden.

In a few weeks, I'll make every effort to report for jury duty with a good attitude. When I get home, I'll share my day with Jessie and take pride in knowing I performed my civic duty. Who knows, the next time life throws me branches, I just might build another fort. On second thought, Jessie loves to roast marshmallows, so maybe we'll make a campfire. I'll keep a positive attitude, too, even if my marshmallow catches fire and turns black before I blow it out.

Sweeter than Icing

I'll remember this birthday. I had a fine day with the usual goodies – a few presents, a birthday kiss from Mattie, lots of birthday cards, a big hug from Jessie, and a cake. Well, sort of. Before I dive into the icing of this story, I want to emphasize that the cake is not the most important part of my birthday. In other words, I'm not complaining about my "sort of" birthday cake.

A couple of weeks before my birthday, Jessie and I were shopping when she spotted Colorflame candles. I had never heard of these, but for *only* $2.75 I could purchase a box of 12 candles that burn with red, purple, green, blue, and orange flames. Jessie quickly gave her sales pitch. "Dad, these candles are awesome!"

I must admit, I thought they were pretty neat, and they even came with a dozen candleholders, but I couldn't see spending 25 cents per candle, plus tax, no matter what primary or secondary color they would display. Somehow, though, Jessie's eyes twinkled exactly the right color, and a few moments later, I stood at the cash register with my wallet open.

Each year, Mattie and Jessie make a Jell-O cake for my birthday. They bake a white cake. After it cools, they add boiling water to gelatin powder. Next, Jessie stabs the cake with a fork and pours the fruit-flavored liquid into the holes and it seeps into the cake. For icing, they mix powdered sugar and Cool Whip. I make a wish, blow out a few candles, and we dive in. That's how it's supposed to work.

A week before my birthday, Mattie asked if I would pick up Cool Whip when I did my grocery shopping. I knew the plan. Yum, yum. I responded, "I'd be glad to, Dear." So I added Cool Whip to my grocery list and purchased it during my regular shopping trip.

Two days before my birthday, Mattie, after checking the pantry, said, "I thought Jessie said we had a white cake mix. I don't see any. Would you mind picking up a box? And if you want a certain Jell-O flavor, please buy that, too." I replied, "No problem, Dear," and purchased the cake mix and cherry-flavored Jell-O that evening.

The day before my birthday, Jessie began to sniffle and cough. I grumbled to Mattie, "Oh no, she's coming down with a cold." When I woke Jessie for school on my birthday, sure enough, she had a cold. The plan called for Jessie to bake my cake when she returned home from school to give it time to cool. Then, when Mattie came home from work, Mattie and Jessie would mix the Jell-O and make the icing.

When I picked Jessie up from school, I could tell her cold had worsened. She loves to work in the kitchen, so I knew she felt lousy when she turned down the opportunity to bake my cake. She suggested I call Mattie and ask her to come home to bake it because she didn't feel up to it. Rather than bother Mattie, I decided to bake my own cake while Jessie rested. No problem; this stay-at-home dad's job description covers just about everything.

Mattie came home tired. Jessie's cold, on her scale of one to ten, had hit twelve. The birthday boy had a white cake, but no fork holes, Jell-O, or icing. Mattie offered to finish the cake, but I said, "Let's just celebrate my birthday tomorrow."

The next day, Jessie felt better. She stabbed the cake, and with a little help from her mom, finished it. Jessie placed Colorflame candles in their holders and inserted them into the icing. She ran around the house and turned out all the lights. Then I struck a few matches to light my candles. As Mattie and Jessie sang "Happy Birthday," I stared at the colorful flames and made a wish before blowing them out.

I'm glad I bought the candles. I didn't mind making two trips to the grocery store for the ingredients. Heck, it didn't even matter that I had to bake my own cake and didn't get to taste it on my birthday. The smiles of Mattie and Jessie were sweeter than the icing on the cake. It wasn't sort of a good moment, it was a great one.

The Humbling Workout

Inhale. Pull inward. Not even close. Lie down on the bed. Inhale again. Minor grunt and pull harder. Failed a second time. Deeper inhale. Major grunt and pull with all my might. Success! I buttoned my pants.

Okay, maybe the pants I managed to close hadn't been worn in a number of years, but still, I questioned, "How did this happen?" I have a bookshelf full of tennis trophies proving my athletic prowess. I still play tennis once or twice a week and walk the dog daily. I have jump rope and hula-hoop contests with my fourth grader. We also play basketball, soccer, tennis, and volleyball together. How did these extra pounds end up around my waist?

I have a few sneaking suspicions, beginning with "Two Donut Thursdays." Hey, Mattie needs gas in her car and the donut shop is on the way. I also love ice cream, which is my comfort food at the end of each day. As soon as Jessie's head hits the pillow, I open the freezer, pull out the half-gallon container, and start dipping. Challenging days require an extra dip … or two.

Recently, Mattie lost 6 pounds. Is it possible the pounds could have jumped off of her onto me while we were sleeping? Or maybe it's my intake of licorice, which keeps me alert while I'm typing or driving on long trips. The bag claims in big letters that it's a "low-fat snack."

My final hypothesis is that my metabolism has slowed down. According to WebMD, "for most people, metabolism slows steadily after age 40." Though Jessie keeps this 54-year-old dad active, there's only so much she can do. Or is there?

"Dad, I can help you lose weight!" I erred when I thought trying to get my pants shut was going to be the hardest part of my day. After hearing about my waistline problem, Jessie had the laptop computer set up in the living room in a heartbeat. "Dad, it's time for your cardiovascular workout."

Before beginning the workout, I remembered something I had seen on a recent stroll with the dog. My neighbor stopped at the end of the street, dropped down, and did 30 push-ups. As he walked past me, I said, "Wow, I haven't done that many push-ups in 30 years," but I thought "Show-off!"

Now, I might not be the poster boy for a gym, but felt confident I could handle a little nine-minute workout. Besides, it would be a fun daddy-daughter activity. I wasn't even intimidated when a disclaimer popped up on the computer screen that suggested consulting a healthcare professional before proceeding.

Without going into all the details, three words summed up the nine-minute workout. "It wasn't pretty." I knew at about minute three that the next six minutes were going to challenge every ounce of my mental and physical toughness. I continued on with a sense of peace that at least I taught Jessie at an early age to dial 9-1-1 for medical emergencies. By workout's end, my flushed face pressed against the living room carpet, but I had enough lung capacity to gasp to Jessie, "Don't call for an ambulance."

As my face regained its natural color and my breathing resumed its normal pattern, I realized my stud-muffin days have passed. Mattie says those days were all in my head anyway. Now, I have to worry about the muffin top that's starting to hang out over the waistline of my jeans. Apparently, I need to make lifestyle changes involving fewer sweets and more physical activity. Luckily, I have Jessie and her various exercise programs and ideas. She already has the next video planned for our workout – belly dancing.

I'll be sure to read any disclaimers that pop up before I do any shimmying. I might buy a bigger ice cream scoop, too.

Chapter 5

Holiday MoMENts

Relax – With all that energy expended, it's good we have the holidays to relax. Hmmm, maybe "relax" isn't the right word. Rejuvenate? Nah, I don't think that's it either. Somehow "relax" and "rejuvenate" would not be words I use to describe holidays. Maybe it's because I have to work so hard to romance my valentine each year, but I don't think it's just me. With all of the pressures and expectations of the holidays, sometimes it's a struggle to remain calm, joyful, and present in the moment. But holidays are a great time to reflect on what is important, to remind our friends and family how much we love them, and to rejoice.

So, I'm trying to relax, and encouraging other parents to do the same. Color, have picnics, and let the kids decorate – even if you, like us, end up with a disco ball in your nativity set. The decorations, like other aspects of the holidays, don't have to be perfect to be wonderful.

I Love Me … and My Family

Before we know it, the 12,000-pound ball will descend over Times Square. Millions of people will kiss and sing Auld Lang Syne to kick off a new year, which brings a new set of days – 366 this year – to meet our New Year's resolutions.

My resolution for the New Year: I'm going to love me. No, I'm not having self-esteem issues. I like myself, even though my pants are getting tighter, my posture isn't as straight, and flecks of silver are mixing in with my remaining brown hairs.

"If my girls are happy, I'm happy." I say this all the time, as taking care of Mattie, Jessie, and Sadie gives me joy. Of course, I'm responsible for my happiness, too – and for taking care of myself.

A few days ago, I took time to go to the doctor. For the past several months, I've woken up with a plugged ear. Usually, it opens up quickly, so I've tolerated it. Who has time to go to the doctor? I have a wife, daughter, and dog to care for, all while trying to squeeze in a writing career.

Apparently, some wax had built up in my left ear. The nurse sprayed warm water into it as I held a plastic container to catch the water and ear wax that flushed out. The nurse asked me, "Are you okay?" I responded, "Yeah, as long as I don't see water coming out of my right ear when you're spraying it into my left one." The wax proved stubborn, so the nurse added drops to loosen it up. While we waited for the drops to take effect, she pulled a little wax out of my right ear.

As I drove home from my ear tune-up, my mind raced with thoughts. With my wax-free ears, I wouldn't need to tell Mattie or Jessie to "please turn up the TV" as often. Yet, maybe, due to Jessie talking excessively, which happens on occasion, and Sadie barking loudly, which happens frequently, I might miss my ear wax. I felt confident I'd still have "selective hearing" (it's a husband thing). But mostly, I thought, "Wow, why didn't I go to the doctor sooner?"

As I drove home, I pondered other things I should have done sooner. Before I reached my driveway, I calculated that it had been five months since I played tennis, my outlet for stress and favorite form of exercise. And yes, more comfort foods have snuck into my diet, not just "Two Donut Thursdays."

If I'm going to be around to see, enjoy, and be part of my family's happiness, I need to take better care of me. I need to love me, so I can continue to love others. Sometimes I'll need to say "No," not only to ice cream and donuts, but also to demands on my time. I must also get more sleep, as I've been sacrificing zzz's in my attempt to steal extra minutes from my nights to pad my days.

I haven't completed my list of New Year's resolutions yet, but here's a good start: Adequate sleep —

seven hours instead of six or less. Exercise – tennis once a week. Appropriate choices from the basic food groups (but I can't give up "Two Donut Thursdays" or ice cream as a bedtime snack). Okay, I didn't say I'd meet all my resolutions. But I'm going to try to do better, because I love me, and I love my family. A gym I drive by daily has a sign out front that reads "Strive for progress, not perfection."

In 2016, I'll schedule my annual physical. Recently, I had a colonoscopy, so I'm okay there for a few years. But whether it's getting exercise, a physical, or a colonoscopy, it's important to set aside time to care for our bodies – so our bodies can care for (and try to keep up with) our children.

Before the ball drops over Times Square, I'll walk into Jessie's bedroom and kiss my sleeping angel on the forehead. Then Mattie and I will probably watch the celebration in New York from bed as we wait for the ball to descend. At midnight, I'll kiss Mattie and then listen to Auld Lang Syne with my wax-free ears. Then I'll close my eyes and give thanks for another year of being there for my family.

Expressions of Love

Valentine's Day is February 14. Hey, Mattie, could I just vow my love for you here and skip romancing you with gifts and poems? I love you! Will you be my valentine? I already know your answer, "Try a little harder." Oh well, it was worth a shot.

Each year, I romance Mattie on the days leading up to Valentine's Day. She finally gives in and consents to be my valentine near midnight on February 14. For the past couple of years, Jessie has helped me convince her mom that I'm a great choice for a valentine, so Mattie has caved in a few hours earlier than usual. It never hurts to have a little extra help.

Thinking of love reminds me of my wonderful neighbors in South Carolina. Mattie and I have been trying to sell our house there since 2007. Though we've been gone for almost five years, our South Carolina neighbors – Jack and Louise, Mike, Sue, Joe and Peggy, and Tarina –continue to shower us with love.

Jack and Louise live next door. Jack lets realtors, prospective buyers, and repairmen into the house. He replaces light bulbs. From time to time he emails pictures, such as our tulips blooming in the spring, a beautiful snowfall, and, once, pictures of a tree that fell on our garage. I enjoyed the tulip pictures a whole lot more. Louise has shared several delicious meals with me during my trips to take care of the house.

Mike owns a nearby tennis club. During one of my trips, I mentioned to him that I planned to take my weight set back to Statesboro. To my surprise, he showed up at my house a few minutes later to help me dissemble and load it onto my truck.

Sue babysat 2-year-old Jessie the day the moving truck came. Jessie got her fingernails painted for the first time, while Mattie and I furiously finished packing and the movers loaded the truck. This past summer, Sue entertained Jessie by feeding fish in the lake with bread in between her toes, something I wasn't about to do.

Joe happened to be driving by when we found ourselves locked out of our house a few days after we bought it. In his truck, he had both a phone book and a cell phone, which we used to call the locksmith. That's when we started calling him "Angel Joe." Joe's wife, Peggy, never misses an opportunity to watch Jessie when we are in town.

Although our neighbors have always been wonderful, I couldn't believe what I saw when I pulled in the driveway for my last visit. Tarina, a physician, had planted pansies and daises in our flowerbeds at her own expense and had been watering them regularly. This is the same Tarina who came to our house at midnight when Jessie came down with her first ear infection. She didn't leave until Jessie was resting comfortably.

We teach Jessie that it is better to give than to receive. We have been blessed to be surrounded by cheerful givers in Seneca, and now here in Statesboro, people who express love through kind deeds and know how to make any day feel like Valentine's Day.

Expressions of love make the world a better place. Not to mention, they may help you snag a valentine. Mattie, will you be my valentine yet? Heck, it didn't hurt to give it one more try.

Tails of Love

"Mattie, will you be my valentine?" On February 1, I'll pose this question to my wife of almost 30 years. She'll be noncommittal. Over the 14 days that follow, I'll continue to romance Mattie with poems, small gifts, and various acts of service in an effort to convince her that I'm the valentine for her. Finally, late in the evening on Valentine's Day, Mattie will say "Yes, I'll be your valentine *this year.*"

We started playing this game before we were married. It's not easy to come up with fresh rhymes 14 times each February, even for a writer. A wiser man would have quit years ago. I thought things would get easier when Jessie was younger. She joined in the efforts to convince her mom to select me. Unfortunately, my proponent turned into my opponent during the last few years, as Jessie started lobbying for Mattie to choose her. Could Valentine's Day get any more challenging? Surprisingly, yes.

Jessie is now also campaigning on behalf of Sadie, who joined in the competition to be Mattie's valentine. Jessie sends emails and hand-written notes, some stamped with an inked dog paw, and often with drawings or cutout hearts, signed by the dog. One example read, "Dear Woofy Mom, I love you! Be my Woofitine." How can I compete with dog love?

Recently, though, I witnessed a beautiful display of love that didn't involve poetry, flowers, chocolate … or removing ink from a dog's paw. The love came from Jessie's head as she had 9 inches of hair cut and donated to an organization that makes wigs for women fighting cancer. Of course, I had my camera and camcorder to capture Jessie's haircut. Mattie joined us from work. Even Jessie's grandmother, who happened to be in town, came to watch. The beauty salon should have sold tickets.

As the hairdresser formed two tight ponytails to prepare Jessie's hair for the scissors, I observed a mother holding her 1-year-old son in the chair next to Jessie's. The little guy did pretty well until the hairdresser broke out her noisy shaver, which resulted in a few tears. My eyes moved back and forth between the two young customers. The one received a slight trim, while the other lost a lot of hair.

My mind wandered back to the scene in our kitchen years ago, when Mattie gave Jessie her first haircut. At the time, I highly questioned her decision to do it herself, as I remembered Mattie's only haircutting experience, the "trim" she gave our first dog. The long strands on the Sheltie's hindquarters touched the ground and dragged leaves into the house. That didn't happen after Mattie made some lopsided cuts and then had to even them out. The remaining fur barely covered the poor dog's behind.

Thank goodness dogs can't talk ... oh that's right, mine is competing to be my wife's valentine.

The hairdresser cut off Jessie's two ponytails and carefully placed them in a plastic bag, then posed with our pretty, shorthaired girl for some pictures. At home, we addressed a padded envelope and slid in the bag containing Jessie's hair, along with her name and address. Many times, I've left the post office feeling happy that in a few days, a card, letter, or photo I had mailed would make someone's day. I won't soon forget the feeling I had when I mailed my daughter's hair. Love can be expressed in many ways.

I'm confident that in the days ahead, I'll overcome my daughter's rivalry, as well as my dog's, and win Mattie's heart for another Valentine's Day. And when I hug my valentine this year, I'll think about other husbands who are thankful they can hug their wives, regardless of how much hair either spouse has.

Leprechauns, Pots of Gold, and Clovers

Prior to St. Patrick's Day last year, my 9-year-old daughter came home from school and asked to have a picnic. Jessie loves picnics.

We tossed two blankets in the yard and placed two lawn chairs on top of them. I relaxed in one of the chairs while Jessie prepared our picnic. She likes to be in charge of the menu and entertainment. About 10 minutes later, Jessie called for assistance. She carried the basket of snacks and a few sheets of paper. I grabbed the crayons and markers. Of course, Sadie joined us; it wouldn't be a picnic without Sadie. A few seconds later, Jessie's feet were free of socks. We munched on pretzels and raisins and shared a can of Orange Crush soda a friend gave her for Valentine's Day.

My future third-grade teacher (Jessie's current career aspiration) then distributed my first assignment, a St. Patrick's Day maze. She had downloaded the maze from a teaching website and printed copies for each of us. We raced to see whose leprechaun would reach the pot of gold first. Jessie won.

My second assignment involved a coloring sheet that pictured a pot of gold. I like to color; however, my aspiring teacher gave me the following writing prompt, "If I saw a leprechaun, I would ...." Instead of coloring the pot of gold, Jessie asked me to write my answer inside the pot. My writer friends know I'm not a big fan of writing on demand. I was ready to object, but noticed Jessie had already started to write on her copy, so I hastily began my assignment.

Jessie finished well ahead of me. She wrote, "If I saw a leprechaun I would ask him nicely to give 1,000 million dollars to help find a cure for cancer."

Jessie's answer clearly beat mine, but for writing on demand, I did okay. "If I saw a leprechaun, I would say, 'Hi, my name is Patrick. No, St. Patrick's Day was not named after me, though I'm a kind and loving man. I already found my pot of gold. I have a beautiful wife, daughter, and dog. I'm a blessed man.'"

Jessie then handed me my third assignment, a coloring sheet with the words "HAPPY ST. PATRICK'S DAY" surrounded by green clovers. Finally, my chance to color. I searched for a green crayon.

Teacher Jessie had a different lesson plan. She gave me the writing prompt, "If I found a pot of gold, I would spend it on," with my answer to be written on the back of the paper. I wanted to raise my hand and ask for a bathroom pass, but I knew my request would be denied. Like before, Jessie finished well before me. She chewed on a pretzel stick and waited patiently.

Jessie's been campaigning for another dog, so her answer didn't surprise me. "If I found a pot of gold I would spend it on one more dog. It would be a Havanese. I would spend the rest on books."

I've been campaigning for a man cave, a quiet area to focus on my writing. I wrote, "If I found a pot of gold, I would spend it on building a man cave. It would be a luxurious man cave with all the amenities a famous writer would have. I'd have state-of-the-art office equipment. I would install a bell on my desk. I would ring it to have my assistant bring me a snack or whatever else I need. For now, I'm happy with my man chair."

As I reflect on our St. Patrick's themed-picnic, these thoughts stand out. Jessie will make an outstanding teacher. Her best chance for a Havanese is to find a pot of gold; they're expensive little puppies. I'm getting better at writing on demand, though I still don't enjoy it. Wouldn't it be wonderful if Jessie found a leprechaun who could fund research to cure cancer?

Finally, I need to accept that my luxury man cave, with assistant, is not likely to happen. But hey, with the extra writing practice, maybe I'll become a famous author and can upgrade to a man sofa.

A Wagon Filled with Memories

"Let's clean out the garage today." How did this statement come from my mouth? If I had typed these words, I could have highlighted the sentence and pressed the delete key before anyone saw it. However, like all words, once they're spoken in front of witnesses, you can't take them back. Mattie quickly seconded the idea, as this project had been on my Honey-Do list for quite some time. Jessie made it unanimous.

I then pointed out what I saw as the most likely problem in tackling this massive project – too many supervisors. I emphasized, "We can only have one supervisor!" Jessie's hand shot up from the kitchen table, at which point I realized that I either need to raise my hand faster or yell "me" when I end select sentences.

Okay, besides attempting to tackle this project with two supervisors – yes, Mattie also likes to lead – I knew our different personalities would enter into play. There's Mr. Sentimental (me). I know Jessie can't use her pink ball glove anymore, but we have to keep it – forever. Then, there's Mrs. Clutterfree (Mattie). "We haven't used it in the last five years. Take it to Goodwill." Finally, there's Miss Open Every Box. "What's in that box? Let's pull that box down." We weren't into the cleaning project very long before I concluded that a trip to the dentist for a root canal would have been more fun.

At day's end, I was pleased with the progress my two supervisors and I had made. The car would have to stay parked in the driveway for the night as the garage floor was covered with *everything*, but family harmony is more important. Overall, though, I thought we worked well as a team. Did we have differences of opinion? Yes. Did I go to bed exhausted? You bet. Will I get to be the supervisor for day two of garage cleaning? Like Jessie's odds of getting a horse for her next birthday, not a chance.

Though I had been dreading this huge project, my two supervisors and I shared some special times. Mattie and I pulled out possessions we hadn't seen in years and Jessie had never seen. One box contained love letters and poems I wrote to Mattie before we were married. Jessie and Mattie laughed when I read one letter aloud. I can't believe I wrote such mushy stuff and it worries me a little that I have no recollection of writing it.

Jessie said she could part with her tiny red wagon. Mattie, Mrs. Clutterfree, said, "We can't give that away. That's where Jessie had her apple sales." Jessie's preschool class for 2-year-olds took a field trip to an apple orchard. I had fun picking apples with Jessie and we filled her bag in no time. Of course, Daddy picked the high ones. When we got home, we decided to have an apple sale. We made a sign: Apples For Sale – Only 25 cents. Jessie loaded her apples into her little red wagon and set up shop with her newly acquired red and green inventory. I cleared a small bookshelf in our guest room and it made a perfect display for Jessie's merchandise. We had so much fun selling and buying apples, learning about money, giving change, and talking about how to run a successful business that we repeated the process after Halloween with Jessie's trick-or-treat candy.

My most sentimental moment came when I pulled a sign away from the wall and found half of a pink, plastic Easter egg. Jessie hid plastic eggs long after Easter had ended. To make hide-and-seek last longer, she split each egg in half. I, Mr. Sentimental, said, "Oh, I'm keeping this." Of course, Mrs. Clutterfree's immediate response was, "Trash!" Now, I admit, a half of a plastic egg covered with dust and spider webs doesn't make the best keepsake, but I'm not a hoarder. Okay, maybe I'm a hoarder of memories.

The garage cleanup will probably take several more days. Will I find the other half of the pink egg? Mattie better hope not, because if I do, I'm saving it. I'll store it in Jessie's tiny red wagon.

The Eggshausting Hunt

"Dad, you can't stop until you find them all." Jessie spoke these words during last year's Easter egg hunt. Why did Mattie and I teach Jessie not to quit when the going gets tough?

Before I discuss the egg collection, let me describe how Jessie ended up hiding 43 eggs for me to find. I carried the large box containing her plastic eggs from the garage to the kitchen. Jessie said, "I'll go through them and pull out my favorite ones." I responded, "No more than 36," thinking that would be plenty for the Easter Bunny (me) to hide.

Jessie sifted through the box and pulled out her favorites. The variety of colors, shapes, and sizes in the keeper pile made an impressive collection. Jessie counted them and said, "86." Before I could repeat, "No more than 36," my quick thinker said, "I know, I'll hide half of them and you can hide the other half."

As an experienced husband (married 30 years) and dad (10 years), I learned long ago to choose my battles wisely. I did a quick math calculation and to me, 43 eggs versus 36 didn't seem like a big deal. I agreed to the negotiated egg-count terms. "Negotiated" sounds better than "I caved." A daughter's fluttering eyelashes are hard to resist, especially when she's wearing an Easter dress.

Egg hiding sure has changed over Jessie's young life. In her early years, I hopped around the yard and hid both plastic and painted eggs. Jessie always enjoyed finding them, except for the one the dog found first and ate. However, before too long, Jessie wanted the egg-hiding role.

I never imagined I'd have to fight to keep my job as Easter Bunny; I have excellent qualifications. At 6'5", I can hop a lot higher than Jessie. Mattie has video footage to prove it. In spite of my superior hopping performance, I've shared the egg-hiding job with Jessie for the past few years. I hid the eggs first, then after Jessie found them all, we reversed roles. However, last Easter, Jessie's 11th, she wanted to go first, so she and Mattie proceeded to the yard with her 43 eggs while I stayed in the house and didn't look. Alone in the house, I came up with the brilliant plan to hide my eggs inside, which struck me as a win-win for both Easter Bunnies.

I must also share one hide-and-seek rule we implemented long ago so the egg hunt would finish before Christmas. The hider can't open things and tuck eggs inside. In other words, the Easter Bunny would never lift the garbage-can lid or open the door to the truck parked in the driveway.

Apparently, Jessie forgot about this standing rule. Luckily, she gave me hints. "You're getting warm, hot, cold, colder." It's good she did, too, because I'd still be looking for a few of them. She hid one egg in a vacant bird's nest inside the birdhouse. She completely covered one egg with pine straw. Somehow, she planted one egg in the spouting at the edge of the roof. Maybe she *can* hop higher than me? Jessie propped another egg (the last one I found) on a tree branch 10 yards into the pine woods behind our house.

My most difficult find, though, was the tiny, pink egg Jessie tucked in the exhaust pipe of our van, which was, technically, out-of-bounds in the garage. Unfortunately, she pushed the egg in too far and it tumbled down the curve in the pipe. I retrieved a flashlight, but couldn't see it. Mattie and Jessie stood in the driveway as I started the car, hoping the egg would come out. I turned the key in the ignition. Mattie said the egg shot out about 10 feet. All outside eggs had been found – not easily, but at least a trip to the mechanic wasn't necessary.

Jessie found the inside eggs with ease. Hey, I followed the rules.

This year, I'll be sure to review the Easter Bunny hiding rules before Jessie heads outside with her basket of eggs. I need to prevent exhaustion issues ... for me and my car.

Take Time to Color

I planned a Saturday full of exciting activities with Jessie. First on the agenda was the local Arbor Day Festival. During the drive, Jessie made me smile as we sat at a traffic light. The vehicle in front of us had a spare tire cover that read, "Life Is Good." Jessie pointed it out and commented, "You say that all the time." I'm glad she's listening.

Jessie had a wonderful time at the festival as she painted, glued, stickered, drew, and even decorated a cookie. I'm not sure which she enjoyed more, decorating the cookie or eating it. Our day was off to a delicious start.

After the festival, I had planned to take Jessie to a college tennis match, and then have a quick lunch, followed by a baseball game on campus. With all the painting, gluing, and cookie eating, we fell behind schedule. I wasn't ready to adjust the day's itinerary quite yet as we only had to pick up our free tree, and then head to the courts. However, there was one other table with a coloring activity we had passed on our walk, adjacent to the free-tree stand. Jessie has lots of coloring books at home, but she wanted to color the photocopied picture of a man planting a tree. I didn't think it would take very long, so we stopped to color before getting our tree.

Two college-aged women handed out the copies for kids to color. Jessie carefully selected colors from the big tray of crayons in the center of the table. As she colored her picture, one of the two women picked up a copy to color, too. She said, "I can't remember the last time I colored."

When she made this comment, I thought of Randy Pausch, a professor who taught at Carnegie Mellon University, who died in 2008 from pancreatic cancer. Prior to his passing, he wrote "The Last Lecture." In the book, he stated that the smell and feel of a crayon takes people back to their childhood dreams. I shared this story with the young woman who was coloring with Jessie. She responded, "My mom reminds me that I'm only 20 and to enjoy life."

That seemed like pretty good advice. I watched patiently as Jessie finished coloring her picture. Then we picked up our two tiny trees.

We didn't make it to the tennis match. We did have a nice lunch and I bought Jessie a cute deer jewelry box at the restaurant's gift shop. The baseball game was great as the home team won 10-1. Near the end of the game, the weather turned cooler. Jessie sat in my lap and I wrapped my jacket around her. I never achieved my childhood dream to be a professional baseball player, but being a pro-dad is even better. Life *is* good.

Back at home that afternoon, Jessie, Mattie, and I planted the two trees in a light rain. Jessie loves to dig and play in the dirt. By the time the trees were planted, she was a mess. Two planted trees equaled two loads of laundry.

As I folded laundry that evening, I mentally replayed the fun day we shared. I would have done only one thing differently. Getting to the tennis match? Nope. Planting trees on a less muddy day? No, again. I wish I had asked for a copy of the coloring page and had taken time to color. Sometimes I need to listen to my own advice. Going forward, instead of rushing through my day, disappointed I'm falling further behind, I'll try to live more in the moment. Life is good.

Labor of Love

Last Labor Day, Jessie and I celebrated the holiday by shopping. I like to shop for bargains – instead, I got more than I bargained for.

Our trip began at the Belk store in the mall. I thought we'd be going to the Girl's department, but Jessie wanted to shop in Junior's. How could this be? "Jessie, we shop in Girl's, like we've always done." Oh how I recall the 2Ts, 3Ts, and the cute little dresses. Junior's Clothing?!

We bought a top, Jessie's first Junior's purchase. As Jessie tried on all kinds of clothing she had picked off the racks, I stood outside the dressing room adjacent to the bikini display. I couldn't help but notice that all the bikinis had padded bras. "I want to go back to the Girl's department!"

After Jessie's purchase, she convinced me to shop for myself. "I'll help, Dad." I pulled a few pairs of swim trunks, shorts, and shirts to try on. Jessie selected a few things for me, too. She stood outside the dressing room while I quickly tried on the items. Up to this point, I had never left Jessie by herself, especially with me in the changing room with my pants down. However, my Junior's-wearing girl assured me, "Dad, I'll be fine." Jessie gave me her opinion as I modeled each selection for her. Wow, talk about reversing roles. Though Jessie didn't want to go to the Girl's department, Dad did. Jessie didn't buy anything; she shops in Junior's now.

Next, we shopped for shoes. I bought a pair of white sneakers. I like white, but Jessie prefers neon-colored shoes. "Jessie, look at this cute pair of white sneakers with a splash of neon." No, she selected tennis-ball yellow sneakers. I almost thought I'd have to go to the van for my sunglasses. The color was one thing, the size another. They were Women's shoes. Junior's clothing and Women's shoes. I'm not ready for this.

Next, we stopped at the Hallmark store. Jessie bought a mug for the dog to give Mattie for Christmas. One can't get the dog-Christmas-shopping out of the way too early.

Time for lunch, and not a minute too soon. We ate at the Sonic a few minutes away. Jessie moved to the front seat to eat her meal and drink her slushy. She took her socks off and threw them backwards, peeking to make sure she hadn't thrown them out the window. She stuck her feet out the sunroof. I smiled as my little girl had returned, if only for a few minutes.

Prior to leaving Sonic, we took a selfie to send to her mom. Jessie texted the photo with a note that read, "I'm staying in the front seat on the way to Office Max (our next destination)."

Mom wrote back, "What???? My baby rides in the back seat!!!!!"

Jessie replied, "NOT NOW. I bought a shirt in the Junior's."

Mom responded, "Get in the back seat and take back the Junior's shirt. You are my baby!"

Three weeks after the shopping trip, Jessie celebrated her 10th birthday. Weren't we just concerned about labor pains? It's hard to believe it's been 10 years of labor ... and love.

A few months after the Labor Day shopping excursion, Mattie and Jessie went shopping for bras ... for Mattie. Jessie helped Mattie this time. They came home with matching panties, bought in Intimate Apparel, not Girl's.

During the drive to school a week later, Jessie asked me to relay a message, "Please tell Mom it's matching panty day." After I dropped Jessie off, I stopped at the donut shop and ordered two glazed donuts, my standard order. I might not be able to share in matching panty day (and don't want to), but I can take comfort in my matching donuts. Something tells me my future holds a number of "matching donut days." But that's okay; I'm sure Jessie will be glad to help me shop for larger pants.

A Special Halloween

Jessie loves to be in charge of decorating for holidays. "I want to decorate all by myself" is something I've heard many times. She enjoys decorating for Christmas best, because we have lots of boxes filled with Christmas ornaments, lights, and bows. However, whether she has many boxes or only one, Jessie has fun and makes the most of her decorating supplies.

On a beautiful Saturday morning three weeks before Halloween, I decided to wash my wife's van. Mattie was returning from a business trip that night, so I thought it would be a nice welcome-home surprise. Jessie likes to help wash cars and anything or anyone the hose will reach.

When Jessie helps wash the family vehicles, she prefers rinsing over scrubbing. As I vacuumed the van's interior, Jessie watered the watermelon plants, air, and grass. Since she likes to be in charge of the water hose, the new nozzle added to the excitement. Of course, Jessie had to try *all* the settings, clicking from one to the next by twisting the plastic nozzle head to achieve a spray, jet, or various other configurations of water flow. Jessie is a lot like her mom. Mattie's brother bestowed upon her the title "Dictator of the Bathroom," when they were growing up together in a one-bathroom house. Jessie is apparently striving to be "Dictator of the Water Hose."

During a snack break, I asked if Jessie would like to decorate for Halloween before her mom got home. She enthusiastically responded, "Yay! May I do it all myself?" I retrieved the box marked "Halloween" from the garage, then left my experienced decorator in charge while I finished the car. Back outside, I enjoyed my freedom to squirt the hose whenever I wanted.

About 30 minutes later, I walked in to *Halloween*. Jessie had taped a foam ghost to my computer. She hung spider webs from the light above my desk. Two stuffed animals, a white ghost and a black cat, peeked out from under the comforter in the master bedroom. If they didn't scare Mattie, the spider attached to the toilet tank would.

When I walked into the living room, I found Jessie at the coffee table, crayon in-hand. She had printed Halloween-themed coloring pages from the computer as she felt the walls needed a little more color.

Jessie and I picked up Mattie a few hours later. I thought we'd surprise her with the clean car and Halloween decorations. Jessie had a different plan. She greeted her mom with a hug and promptly gave her a detailed report.

We had a nice evening, which included Jessie dressing Sadie in her Halloween costume. Jessie decided to be a cat and dress Sadie as a mouse. Sadie didn't mind the gray T-shirt, but I can't say she enjoyed the gray sock pulled over her tail.

Mattie, tired from her trip, went to bed early. I allowed Jessie to stay up past her bedtime to watch a little college football. My two favorite teams lost, one on a last-second field goal. As I crawled into bed, disappointed over the loss, I landed on something. I reached behind me and pulled a ghost and black cat out from under my back. My frown changed to a smile.

I smiled again a few weeks later when a cat, a mouse, and a 6'5" block of moldy cheese greeted trick-or-treaters on our front porch. The cat, who had painted my face and selected my cheese-colored shirt, wore a big grin, too. As for the mouse, she was the cat's best friend.

Jessie already has this year's costumes planned. Recently, Mattie purchased a swimsuit and removed the foam pads from the top. Jessie held each pad to my chest and said, "This year, we're going to be cheerleaders." Here's my response, Jessie, in the form of a cheer. "Give me an N. Give me an O. Give me a W-A-Y. What's that spell? NO WAY! Louder now, NO WAY!"

No matter what costume I wear, or how much my face gets painted, I'm confident we'll have another wonderful Halloween, complete with special decorations. And if our house gets egged, I only need to call Jessie and her trusty water hose.

Half Full

Last fall, I visited Jessie's first-grade class to talk about writing. During my presentation, I also discussed the importance of having a good attitude. I held up a picture of a glass half full of water. The picture's caption read, "Positive Attitude – It changes everything." I asked the students what they thought this picture meant. One boy gave the priceless answer, "It's important that we drink lots of water." I went on to explain that a person with a positive attitude would say the glass is half-full, whereas someone with a negative attitude would say the glass is half-empty.

Shortly thereafter, Jessie and I had a wonderful daddy-daughter date to a Christmas show at our local theater. Prior to the opening act, I waited for her outside of the women's bathroom. I held her magenta, heart-shaped, sequin-covered purse, which didn't go at all with the suit I was wearing. I smiled and said, "thank you" to a man who complimented my purse. Though his "Nice purse" comment didn't bother me, I silently questioned, "Why am I stuck holding Jessie's purse?" Then I thought, "Am I practicing what I preached about keeping a positive attitude?"

During the performance, I frequently glanced over to watch Jessie's facial expressions. I'm not sure which was bigger, her smile or her eyes, as she listened to the music and watched the ballerinas dance. Suddenly, I felt like I was starring in a MasterCard commercial: Lunch at Cracker Barrel – $11; two tickets to the Sunday matinee – $25; viewing the happiness on my daughter's face – priceless.

Of course, not every moment in life can feel like a MasterCard commercial. As Jessie watches me tackle the highs and lows that each day brings, I wonder what attitude she sees. Am I passing on a half-full or half-empty perspective to her watching eyes and listening ears?

In a few weeks, we'll sit around the table to celebrate Thanksgiving and reflect on the past year. It hasn't been a perfect year, but I'll focus on the positive and feel grateful. The house we moved from in 2007 remains unsold. At least, unlike two years ago, a tree didn't fall on it. I received feedback from a respected literary agent that my book manuscript, the one I thought was perfect, still needs work. Yet she suggested how to improve it and invited me to send it to her again when it's finished. We will be celebrating Thanksgiving without a special loved one who died this year, and missing my father, who we lost three years ago. However, we are grateful for the time we had with them and that all of our other family members made it through another year.

The next time I stand in front of a women's restroom holding a shiny purse, I'll smile, knowing that the years for holding daughters and their little-girl belongings pass way too quickly. I will treasure every moment with Jessie, even if I don't look fashionable. My glass isn't half empty. My glass isn't half full. My glass is overflowing.

The Quiet Thanksgiving

A little part of me feels like a hypocrite. Since September 2011, I've written a monthly column that reminds readers to "cherish the moments." Obviously, we cherish some moments more than others, but whether it's a spectacular moment or a stressful one, we don't get the minutes back, so we may as well make the best of them. Yet here I sit, wondering if my present circumstances reflect my own good advice.

In five hours, it will be Thanksgiving Day, and by my own choice I'll be spending it alone. The day will be different from my previous Thanksgivings. I'll have turkey, but it will be of the cold-cut variety, slapped on a foot-long sub roll by a fast-food employee. Every other Thanksgiving, my turkey has been hot, smothered in gravy, and served by someone I love. Even though Thanksgiving is not about the food, I'll miss the freshly made filling and delicious apple pie covered with heaps of whipped cream. Thanksgiving is not about football, either, but after eating 2,000 calories in one sitting, it sure feels good to stretch out on the sofa to watch the games. I like to enjoy part of the action with my eyelids closed and my mouth hanging open, and I'm not usually the only one snoring. As much as I enjoy the food, football, and nap, for me, Thanksgiving is about giving thanks and spending quality time with family.

This year, I'm still thankful, but I chose to spend the holiday without my family, catching up on work. Mattie left with Jessie two days ago. They'll have a wonderful time celebrating Thanksgiving with family in Florida. I had planned to go, but after careful consideration, I opted to stay home. It's just Sadie and me. Sadie would have preferred playing with my relatives' dogs in Florida and getting in on the Thanksgiving turkey. I'm pretty sure she's mad at me. So with Thanksgiving Day only a few hours away, I'm all alone in my dirty house with my angry dog.

I should be thankful; I have everything I wanted – quiet time to work on my manuscript and a bookshelf full of books to read without interruption, other than to toss Sadie her stuffed gorilla now and then. The entire house, every quiet square foot, is mine.

After the past couple of months, I'm due for a little time to be master of my castle, instead of just the "man chair" tucked in the corner of the garage. First, I battled a respiratory infection that required four trips to the doctor's office, cough medicine with codeine, steroids (oral and nasal), penicillin, another kind of antibiotic, a chest x-ray, and an inhaler. I spent seven weeks spitting, hacking, sleeping upright in my recliner, and wondering if I would need to finish my manuscript wearing angel wings. I lost eight pounds. During this time, Mattie had work that required her to go out of town, not once, but twice, and they weren't short trips. She was gone for five days, home for four days, during which my in-laws (whom I love dearly) visited, and then Mattie left for another eight days.

My medicine bottles received more attention than my computer keys. I fell behind on chores around the house. My To-Do list grew longer than Santa's list of good boys and girls, but unlike St. Nick, I don't have a workshop full of elves.

A few days before the planned Thanksgiving trip, I reluctantly informed Mattie of my decision to stay home to work. I added, "I feel like a hypocrite because I tell my readers to cherish the moments. How can I miss Thanksgiving with my family?"

Mattie, knowing that I really needed the time, responded, "It's okay. You need to cherish the moments with yourself right now." Wow, I married well.

As I chew my Thanksgiving sub tomorrow, a number of thoughts will likely cross my mind. This isn't my mother-in-law's turkey. It's okay, Sadie, jump up on the sofa beside me. Most important, I can't wait for Mattie and Jessie to return. My man chair works just fine; I don't need a whole house to myself. Yet I will also be thankful for the peace and quiet, something we all need at times. That doesn't make me a hypocrite.

Thanksgiving Day 2014 update: It turned out that the sub place closed for Thanksgiving. Fortunately, the Chinese restaurant didn't. I enjoyed my meal, though it wasn't nearly as good as my mother-in-law's turkey.

The Most Wonderful Time

Life is hectic enough with the day-to-day stuff. Each day, I add more items to my To-Do list than I check off. Will I ever catch up? It's unlikely. And then it happens — Christmas rolls around. Shopping, decorating, traveling ... collapsing. I sarcastically sing, "It's the Most Wonderful Time of the Year."

Conversely, Jessie plays Christmas music in July. Around September, she asks, "How many days until Christmas?" So I need to take off my "Bah Humbug" hat and find my joyous one.

Right after Thanksgiving last year, Jessie asked, "When can we decorate for Christmas?" A few minutes later, Jessie inquired, "When are we going to get a tree?" Since we weren't going to be home for Christmas, I suggested we forego the tree and just put out the nativity set. Not to mention, it's a hectic time for my wife's work, so I knew Mattie would be unavailable to assist.

I decided to get into the Christmas spirit. This sounds better than "I gave in." Jessie and I set up the nativity set first, one that took Mattie over 10 years to select as she wanted to find the perfect one. It's fragile. But Jessie wanted to arrange all the pieces. I think I said, "Be careful," with each piece I handed to her. She did a fantastic job organizing it. At the end, she tucked her battery-operated disco ball behind the angel, as she wanted the scene to be spectacular. I think it's safe to say that not too many households' nativity scenes contained Joseph, Mary, Baby Jesus, and a rotating disco ball. However, I agreed the colored lights rotating behind the manger scene did add a certain flare without detracting from the beauty and symbolism of the display.

The next day, Jessie and I went tree shopping. We walked down one aisle and up the next. I pulled out four or five 5' to 6' trees and stood them up for Jessie to inspect. "We need a bigger tree, Dad." Jessie and I moved to the row with 6' to 7' trees. Just when I thought, "This is going to take forever," Jessie said, "It's perfect!" to a Douglas fir just under 7' tall. Jessie immediately named our tree "Sally." I left home with Jessie and returned with Jessie and Sally.

The following day, I retrieved all the boxes marked "Christmas" from the garage. Jessie immediately went to work decorating. Once, I came in from the garage to find five red-velvet bows hanging from the light fixture above my desk. The bows' tails were almost touching my computer and were within two feet of my nose when I typed. Still, I had to admit my new work environment brought a smile to my face.

Next, Jessie and I wrapped Sally in lights, another memorable experience. Jessie did not quite grasp the concept (or maybe she did but chose not to apply it) that lights need to gradually descend from top to bottom. It had to be a Christmas miracle, because somehow Sally ended up with lights covering her.

Then, Jessie enthusiastically unwrapped the ornaments, which we had carefully packed away the previous year. One special and fragile ornament recorded Jessie's tiny footprint in plaster. It had taken great effort for Mattie and me to hold her foot still enough to make it for her first Christmas. I asked Jessie to hand it to me. The imprint was only 3" long and 1 ½" wide. Where did my baby go? I know it wasn't a grenade, but I handled it like one.

As Sally became full of ornaments, Jessie concluded, "We need a bigger tree." We finished decorating and then sat in the dark admiring our work. The bright parts with an abundance of lights and the dark spaces without lights all looked good behind the scores of handmade ornaments and souvenirs of our travels and past Christmases together.

As we packed things away in January, I smiled, happy I had invested the time, energy, and expense. Something tells me we'll do it all over again next December. Before too long, I'll hear Jessie say, "Dad, it's time to get a tree. Let's get a real big one this year." But whether we bring home a Peggy, Jane, Susan, or another Sally, I'll remember Christmas is a most wonderful time to cherish.

The Best Gifts

I'm not a big fan of Black Friday, Cyber Monday, or any of the shopping days leading up to Christmas. Though I enjoy giving gifts, the problem is, "What do you get year after year for loved ones who have everything they need?" Even buying presents for Jessie is becoming more of a challenge. No Jessie, you won't be getting a horse for Christmas.

What to buy? Rush to purchase. Stand in long lines. Time to wrap. Too few presents. Too many presents? Big credit card bills in January. More long lines to return gifts. I'm not trying to impersonate Scrooge, but "Bah Humbug!" We all know the holiday season is about love, peace, and goodwill. Why do we drive ourselves crazy?

Speaking of love, and crazy, after a relaxing night of tennis a few weeks ago, I stopped for dinner at a local restaurant. Through the years, I've heard waitresses use many different terms of endearment, like "Darling," "Hon," and "Sweetie." However, when the 20-something waitress delivered my double steakburger and said, "Here you go, my love," I thought I heard her wrong. "My love?" Heck, I've been married over 30 years and I don't even get a "My love, would you please take out the garbage?"

I enjoyed my meal, and then paid with a credit card. When the waitress handed my card back, she said, "Here you go, my love." I gave her a 20 percent tip.

Of course, I drove straight home and playfully bragged to Mattie that a woman more than 20 years my junior called me "my love" – twice. Mattie rolled her eyes, not a bit concerned, and told me to get over myself. Mattie keeps me humble.

However, I couldn't let the fun end. I emailed my wise writing buddy, Jan, to see if she had ever heard a waitress use this expression. Jan felt "my love" was the server's go-to term for customers, rather than a special name for a sweat-soaked tennis player, but suggested I enjoy the moment anyway.

She pointed out that when working for tips, using terms of endearment is a good strategy. Hey, it worked with me. Jan, a few years older than me, also noted, "the waitress will be glad she started using terms of endearment when she was young, because age has a way of making the use of them a necessity!"

Ah – age. Yes, time zooms by quickly. Which brings me back to Christmas shopping. Do I want to waste my precious minutes fretting over presents? No! The best presents aren't tangible anyway (though Jessie thinks a very tangible horse would make a fantastic gift). I'll take family hugs in the kitchen with the dog sandwiched between Mattie, Jessie, and me. Massaging Mattie's feet, propped on my lap, as we laugh together at a TV show. Holding hands during walks. Hearing kind, supportive words – daily terms of endearment like "my love" – from my wife. These are the best gifts, ones that fill my days with joy.

With that said, I'm not Ebenezer Scrooge, and I agree it's nice to have a few presents to open, especially for children. Last Christmas, I printed out a couple of pages from the Save the Manatee Club and let Jessie select a manatee to adopt. She chose a 3-year-old named Squeaky, the youngest manatee in the adoption program from Blue Spring State Park in Florida. I thought she'd enjoy this present, because we visit the park to look for manatees at least once a year. I was surprised, however, that it turned out to be her favorite gift. Go figure.

We asked about Squeaky on our last trip to Blue Spring State Park, but she hadn't been spotted in the springs. We hope to see her next time. I can already hear Jessie shouting "Hi Cutie" at her adopted manatee. We just have to hope this term of endearment doesn't go to Squeaky's head.

Love, peace, goodwill, and helping an endangered species. They all beat standing in long lines and trolling online stores, and cost a lot less than stall rent and food bills for a horse.

Chapter 6

Father MoMENts

I am Dad – Prior to becoming Mr. Mom, I had a professional career, working as a banker, an accountant, and an internal auditor. Although I experienced numerous joys and challenges in those jobs, the job I hold most dear is that of "Dad."

Am I a "Superdad?" Do Superdads need help to change a light bulb? Do Superdads get tired and grouchy? Do Superdads throw up on sailboats? Apparently, I'm not a Superdad, but I can be a present dad who is always there for my child … except on boats.

A Father's Pride

Pride. We all have it, although some have more than others. For example, I'm not one of those prideful guys who, when lost, refuses to stop for directions. I stop and ask because I hate to waste a single one of the 1,440 minutes in my day.

Unfortunately, a recent house repair took its toll on my pride. I couldn't change a light bulb. Before you judge, let me provide details. The two light bulbs in our hallway fixture burned out. Not a problem, I thought, as I only need to undo one screw, let the glass globe drop down, and replace the bulbs. I don't even need a ladder, as I'm tall enough to reach the ceiling. It should have been a simple fix.

The problem occurred when, after I removed the screw holding up the decorative glass globe that covers the light bulbs, the globe remained firmly in place. I tried everything to get the globe down. When lefty-loosey didn't work, I tried righty-tighty. I sprayed WD-40 between the glass globe and the fixture frame. Using a screwdriver, I tried to pry the frame away from the glass globe. That procedure cracked a small piece off of the frame, but I persevered. Using rubber jar grippers for better hold and standing on a stool to generate extra leverage, I struggled with it for 10 more minutes.

I'm aware of the proverb "Pride goeth before a fall." But by this point, I didn't care if I fell off the stool. I just didn't want to be known as the guy who's too stupid to change a light bulb. Now might be a good time to mention my father-in-law is a retired electrician.

Eventually, I ran out of patience, swallowed my pride, and asked Mattie for help, knowing full well that if she got the globe off, a whole list of folks were going to hear about it. She struggled with it briefly and gave up. Still feeling confident that I'm smarter than a glass globe, I came up with a new plan. I retrieved a chair for my 5'3" wife. Mattie stood on the chair and held the exterior frame, while I stood on the stool trying to turn the globe. It wasn't a proud moment, as we talked about the shame of admitting that between the two of us, we couldn't change a light bulb. The globe didn't budge.

I swallowed a bit more pride and called the handyman, Tory, who did some electrical work on the same fixture last year when it emitted sparks and smoke. I remembered the globe had stuck a bit for him, too, but he got it down. The telephone felt like it weighed 20 pounds when I picked it up. I dialed his number, posed my question, and then waited for his laughter – I mean answer. He was kind, but offered no new suggestions. I guess that handymen learn to avoid ridiculing clients to their faces. He told me to call him back if the glass globe proved too much for me (I'm paraphrasing).

I went back and retried all the procedures that had proved unsuccessful earlier. The hallway smelled like a garage, full of the aroma of WD-40. The chipped off piece of the fixture remained on the floor as I continued working the steps until I lost the feeling in my arms from holding them above my head for so long. There's only so much pride I can swallow, so I didn't call Tory back. Plus, he charges $75 to make a service call and I couldn't justify the cost to change a light bulb. I needed to give the problem more thought and come up with another plan.

Coincidentally, over the next week several other things around the house broke, so I could justify the $75 fee for the service call. I called the handyman, rationalizing that I was paying him to perform complicated repairs, not change a light bulb. It took Tory more than five minutes with a screwdriver to pry the globe loose. When he left, I told Mattie, "I'm glad Tory had a tough time with the globe." Jessie, always listening, said, "That's not nice."

Although I was proud of Jessie's response because Mattie and I have taught her not to wish bad things on others, getting a "Be Kind to Others" lecture from my daughter wasn't what my ego needed just then. After all, it had already taken a pretty good beating from the light fixture.

I sat down with Jessie to explain my comment and talk about a man's pride. If that globe had dropped right into Tory's hands … well, let's just say I wasn't anxious to be the butt of the light bulb changing jokes that were sure to come my way.

The story continues. Three days after Tory replaced the two light bulbs, the first burned out. A week or so later the second bulb burned out, so our hallway is once again dark. Apparently the light fixture is defective and will need to be replaced. Although the thought of using my sledgehammer to beat the light briefly entered my mind (after all, it seemed to be out to beat me), I decided to let it go. The hallway remains calmly dark. Heck, it's even romantic.

Eventually my father-in-law will come to town for a visit and replace the fixture. It will probably make him feel good to do it. Come to think of it, I'm glad he'll have an opportunity to use his electrical skills to help his daughter and her family. After all, nothing makes a father prouder than looking good in front of his child.

King

I'm a competitor. In any game, even if it's Chutes and Ladders, I play to win. Because I view April Fools' Day as a competition, it's one of my favorite days of the year. For the first two April Fools' Days at my last job, I was disappointed that it was so easy to win the "King Fool" title, but by the third year I was a marked man. My coworkers tied up my chair, duct-taped my telephone base, handset, and cord to my desk, toilet papered my office, and velcroed my large collection of stress balls to the ceiling. It's hard to claim victory when your possessions are hanging from the ceiling and you can't even pick up the phone to call for help or sit down to plan a counter-attack. Even when I passed the men's restroom and saw that the male figure on the men's restroom sign had my face, I didn't concede. A lesser competitor would have come out of that bathroom waving white toilet tissue to surrender, but not me.

I love competing in all kinds of things, but when it comes to tennis, well, let's just say I dial up the competitive meter. In my younger days, I dived on the courts and crashed into fences all the time. Tennis players should not get concussions. I also agonized over losses more than I should have. After matches, I'd sit in the car replaying points in my head and assessing what I could have done differently. Okay, maybe I moped. Mattie said she knew whether I'd won or lost by how long it took me to come into the house.

I guess I'm wiser now. I've learned that even though winning is much more fun than losing, there are more important things in life.

A few weeks ago, the Mill Creek Tennis Complex held a tennis block party. Among the events was a "King of the Court" competition, which had two age brackets. I should have competed in the over-36 division; however, since only three of us showed up, we decided to play with the guys in the 18-to-35 division. If I had won, I might have put an ad in the newspaper touting the triumph. Unfortunately, youth bested experience.

When I pulled into the garage, I saw Jessie peek through the door. Before I left for the match, I said I was nervous because it had been about five years since I competed in a tennis tournament. I added that it is important not to let fear prevent you from living life, so I was going to play in the event and set a good example for her.

As I walked into the house, Jessie asked, "How did you do?" I told her I had fun, displayed good sportsmanship, and finished third. I picked her up and gave her the biggest of hugs. I wasn't "King of the Court," I said, but something much better. I was "King Dad." Jessie quickly added, "And Momma is queen and Ginger (our previous dog) is princess." I hugged my Princess Jessie again.

My "King Dad" title is so much sweeter than any other title I've won or will ever earn, although I would be pretty excited to win the title of "National Best-Selling Author." In the meantime, Mattie and Jessie, you better not let your guard down on April 1st. I play to win.

Superdad

I'll soon be celebrating my seventh Father's Day as a dad. During those years, I've tried my best to be a "Superdad" for Jessie. I've taught her to read and do math, and how to throw, kick, hit, and catch all kinds of balls. I jogged behind her bicycle, hands outstretched to catch her in case she fell, until she pedaled faster than I could run. I rush to the rescue when she sees spiders and when she has bad dreams, minor cuts, and toilet paper outages. I play along with her games, even though she makes up rules as she goes, and I applaud her imaginative shows in the living room, even when I'd rather take a nap.

Although I strive to be Superdad, I know that I'm not Superman. If I were Superman, though, the ocean would be my kryptonite and the garbage can my Lois Lane. I tend to get sick on boats. Mattie and I went on a whale-watching excursion in San Diego many years ago. On the choppy waters of the Pacific Ocean, Mattie and the other passengers saw whales. I spent the whole trip hugging the garbage can. No one mistook me for Superman that day.

A few years ago, when my garbage can romance in San Diego had faded to a distant memory, Uncle Gary took our family out on his sailboat. Before we boarded, I slipped a plastic bag into my pocket as a precautionary measure, but I didn't think I would need it. After all, we were sailing on a river on a calm day. Soon the wind picked up, though, and as the boat pitched back and forth, my motion sickness, and my breakfast, reemerged. I tried to smile and crack jokes to let Jessie know I was okay. Mattie and I encourage Jessie to take an "I can" attitude and I try to lead by example ... I think I can, I think I can ... Blagh! That time I couldn't. The plastic bag got a serious workout. I'd recommend to other seasick passengers that they double bag.

Mattie took Jessie, who was three years old at the time, down into the boat's cabin so she wouldn't watch me vomit. She told me later that Jessie entertained herself by pretending to throw up in an ice bucket. Children follow their parents' lead.

Jessie has taken many more boat rides since then, but not with Daddy. Luckily, fathers don't have to be Superdads all the time. Grandfathers, uncles, and brothers can be super, too. Mothers, grandmothers, aunts, neighbors, teachers, and friends also enrich our children's lives. Father's Day is a good time to express appreciation to the people who sometimes take on father-like roles.

Jessie, I'll keep trying to be a Superdad with an "I can" attitude. Although, by mutual agreement with Uncle Gary, I won't be sailing with you anymore, I can and will be there for you in other ways. I will encourage you to dream big and maximize your joy each day. I will hold you when you need comforted. There are many places that I can take you and things that I can teach you. I can learn from you, too (like how to divide five cherries on a dessert … three ways). I'll be there to support you as you chart your own path to discover and achieve your life's purpose. Superman, I am not. Superdad? I'll do my best!

Happy Father's Day! I know I'll have a happy one — on solid ground.

What Does the Dad Say?

Jessie loves to watch "Dancing with the Stars." Frequently, she jumps up from the sofa and dances along. Jessie knows that she's the star of our family. During one episode, the cast danced to "The Fox (What Does the Fox Say?)" by Ylvis. The men wore fox costumes. It was entertaining, but the song has a catchy tune that is hard to get out of my head.

The song describes how various animals communicate, and repeatedly uses strings of sounds like "ring-ding-ding-ding-dingeringeding" and "wa-pa-pa-pa-pa-pa-pow." The singer then questions, "What does the fox say?"

Hearing the song made me think of two things. First, it seems like I was just teaching Jessie the different sounds that animals make. How did I go from woof, meow, and tweet to rocks, minerals, and fossils (Jessie's recent science homework)? Her math homework is also becoming difficult. Pretty soon, I may be better off trying to find out what sound the fox makes than helping Jessie solve for x.

More important, the song made me think, "Why ask what the fox says?" The bigger question is, "What does the dad say?"

Don't get me wrong; Jessie, is a well-behaved little girl, but there are times when I think she'd hear me better if I was Taylor Swift, Katy Perry, or Carly Rae Jepsen.

I'm amazed at how quickly she picks up words to songs. However, when I say, "It's cold out today. Wear a long-sleeve shirt and pants," and she comes out in a short-sleeved shirt and skirt, it makes me wonder.

Maybe if I sing my requests, I'll have greater success. I know I won't be able to compete with Taylor Swift or Ylvis, but here goes.

Oh Jessie, when it's time to wake up for school and you pull the covers over your head – What does the dad say? – "Get-get-get-get-get-up-now. Get-get-get-get-get-up-now." When we should have left for school five minutes ago – What does the dad say? – "Hur-hur-hur-hur-hur-ry-up. Hur-hur-hur-hur-hur-ry-up." When it's time to start your homework – What does the dad say? – "Nowie, nowie, nowie, now. Nowie, nowie, nowie, now." When it's time to go to bed – "What does the dad say? – "Off-off-off-off-off-to-bed. Off-off-off-off-off-to-bed."

I could even use this tune when Jessie comes to me with a question I can't answer or a topic better covered by her mother. For example, if Jessie asks for details about where babies come from – What will the dad say? – "Go-go-go-go-ask-your-mom. Go-go-go-go-ask-your-mom." This song will also come in handy when she wants to date a boy before I think she's ready – What will the dad say? – "No-no-no-no-not-a-chance. No-no-no-no-not-a-chance." One day, Jessie may want to move across the country, and though I'll be proud of having raised an independent daughter, – What will the dad say?

– "Boo-hoo-hoo-hoo-Boo-hoo-hoo" (repeat numerous times and then repeat numerous times again).

I don't really care what the fox says. I do care, however, that what I say as a dad falls on attentive ears. There will be many times in the future (as in the past) when Jessie hears all, part, or none of what I said. But each day, whether I say it in words (or sing it), or show it with my actions, I hope Jessie will see, hear, feel, and know – "I'll-always-always-loooovvvve-you! I'll-always-always-loooovvvve-you!"

It seems like I was just dancing with my toddler, her little feet on top of my shoes as she hung on with each step I took. She's growing up so quickly. Today, if Jessie stood on my feet, the steps would go much slower; an extra 80 pounds atop foot bones make it more difficult to move with grace and swiftness. So I conclude this column with one final lyric – My little girl's growing up. What does the dad say? – "Slow-slow-slow-slow-slooooow-down. Slow-slow-slow-slow-slooooow-down."

I Grouchy: A Tired Dad's Story

This morning, Jessie and I sat in her pediatrician's office. As we waited for the doctor, she sat beside me reading, "I Funny: A Middle School Story." I don't know anything about the book, but noticed the grammatically incorrect title. If I had written a story based on my mood at the time, I would have titled it, "I Grouchy: A Tired Dad's Story."

My grouchiness surfaced at the same time as the tiny red spots on Jessie's abdomen, which she scratched fiercely. A similar thing happened about 10 months ago and her doctor had diagnosed it as scabies.

According to About.com Pediatrics, "Scabies is a skin infection caused by an infestation with the microscopic *Sarcoptes scabei* parasitic mite. Although distressing for parents, who associate conditions like scabies and head lice with poor hygiene, scabies is actually fairly common." WebMD adds, "Scabies can affect people of all ages and from all incomes and social levels. Even people who keep themselves very clean can get scabies." I can confirm the "distressing for parents" part and, for the record, we shower daily.

During our visit 10 months ago, Jessie's pediatrician had recommended that the whole family use a lotion to kill the mites. Prior to bedtime that evening, Mattie applied the lotion to Jessie's entire body. How I felt as I crawled into bed, smothered in insecticide lotion, next to

Mattie who was similarly covered, could best be described as, "I miserable."

The anti-mite lotion was only one step. We also needed to kill the mites not on our bodies. I vacuumed the entire house and everything in it (chairs, sofas, carpet, even the dog), plus both cars. I washed twenty loads of laundry, which took three days. I even put Jessie's stuffed animals in the freezer to kill the mites. If someone had opened my freezer and discovered a stuffed monkey staring at them, they might have thought, "I crazy."

Today, as we drove to Jessie's pediatrician, my feelings could be described as, "I sad." Before the doctor's office opened, I had already stripped both beds and had the washer and dryer running. The day is young and already, "I tired."

I don't know what made me say this during the 15-minute drive, as I know how much Jessie hates shots, but I mentioned that at around age 10, children get more vaccinations. This caught Jessie's attention, since her 10th birthday is only eight months away. She whined, "I don't want to get a shot." I clutched the steering wheel, thinking, "I stupid."

So, as I sit in the pediatrician's waiting room, "I grouchy, I sad, I tired, I stupid." Then, I notice a girl a year or two younger than Jessie who is clearly sick. I hear a baby with a bad cough. I look over at Jessie; she's focused on her book. Except for a little itch on her belly, all is well. Gratitude comes rushing in. "I lucky." Since her belly began to itch, I've probably not been the most pleasant person to be around. Mattie would agree. When I get home, I will tell her, "I sorry."

The pediatrician's diagnosis is that Jessie's itch is due to mites from a pet she visited. But this mite is different from the kind she had before; it doesn't survive on humans and goes away without treatment. "I happy."

Reflecting on this day, and another exciting parenting experience, I reach the following conclusions: As parents, we feel lots of intense emotions – I grouchy, I sad, I stupid, I lucky, I sorry, and I happy. Yet, in the pediatrician's waiting room I was reminded, "I blessed."

Jessie just finished reading her book. She told me there's another book in the series titled, "I Even Funnier." I'm not sure what lies ahead in my parenting days, but I'm going to strive for "I Even Smarter," which will be helpful when Jessie becomes a teenager.

But whether I'm going through a joyous parenting moment (I proud) or a challenging time (I worried), one fact remains unchanged. "I Dad," and that's a great feeling.

A Dad's Wall of Joy

I'm not sure if it was Fred, Barney, Wilma, or Betty. It could have been Pebbles or Bamm-Bamm. I do know it was grape flavored and that the children's vitamin should have gone down my daughter's esophagus and not mine.

Each morning, I prepare breakfast for Jessie. If done properly, Jessie eats her Flintstones chewable vitamin, and I swallow my daily vitamin for men. Though the directions on the Flintstones bottle read "Adults and children 4 years of age and over," I'd just as soon swallow the one that better supports my prostate and heart health. However, on two different occasions, I sleepily and without focus took the wrong vitamin. I like orange better than grape.

It seems like I was just watching *The Flintstones* on a black and white TV back in the sixties. With yet another birthday on the horizon, I shake my head in disbelief as to how fast the years have gone by. I've lived lots of exciting phases. I had a successful professional career – 12 years in banking, 4 years in public accounting, and 5 years as an internal auditor. But I wouldn't trade the past 9 years as a stay-at-home dad for anything, even if I had to eat a chewable vitamin every day. Maybe I need to start drinking more caffeine as I try to squeeze in a writing career while tackling my at-home dad responsibilities.

Parenting is immensely joyful, yet it can also be tiring and challenging. Life was a lot simpler watching *The Flintstones*. I have wonderful childhood memories ranging from playing ball to taping comic strips to the kitchen walls.

Now that I'm a parent of a soon-to-be tween, I smile when I glance up from my computer and see evidence of Jessie's happy childhood all over my walls. I remember pre-parenthood, when my office walls held my framed college diplomas, CPA license, and several framed photos that I called my Wall of Fame. My Wall of Fame motivated me with reminders of some of my biggest achievements. One picture flaunted my first victory in a singles tennis tournament. Another showed me on water skis as I attempted to impress Mattie. This undertaking was brave because I didn't know how to swim, but I still jumped in the lake with my life vest on and Mattie's brother ready to assist, if necessary. It must have worked because Mattie married me a few years later.

Another picture showed Mattie and me in Florida on a four-wheeler covered in mud as we drove down "Swamp Road," which was not a road, but an overgrown path through a swamp, with water up to our waists in some parts. Mattie's Uncle Larry took the snapshot, capturing my thrilled expression that we had survived, as the three of us returned to camp from a ride that would have been better suited for a boat. To say I was way outside my comfort zone would be an understatement.

When I look at my walls today, they are a whole lot different. Gone are the diplomas and my Wall of Fame. The wall now holds pictures of a smiling daughter gripping a tennis racquet, reading a book, hugging her dog, bouncing a basketball, finding an Easter egg, even one where she's playing in snow. There are also drawings and colored pictures, which Jessie and I did both individually and jointly. We like to color pictures while picnicking on the garage floor or on a blanket in the back of the pick-up truck parked under the tree in our yard. The pictures are reminders of our quality time together. My walls have changed through the years, just as I have. Though I've been blessed in all stages of my life, the Mr. Mom years have provided me with many of my best memories. I have the pictures to prove it on my "Wall of Joy."

As I continue to work to balance my responsibilities as a father, husband, son, and writer, I realize there will be highs and lows. You won't catch me on water skis or a four-wheeler anymore, as my sense of adventure is different than it used to be and what it takes to impress Mattie has changed. I do hope to keep my Flintstones chewables intake to a minimum. But mostly, I plan to have lots of "yabba dabba doo" times with my family as I color my walls with memories.

Chapter 7

Mother MoMENts

Save me, Mom! – Prior to becoming a parent, I often thanked my mother for the things she did for me. After becoming a stay-at-home dad, I quickly realized I didn't thank her enough. Children bond with their mothers tightly, so moms impact their kids' lives in big and little ways that have profound effects. The lessons moms teach stick; at least, some of them do, and are passed along from their children to their grandchildren. One of my greatest comforts is knowing I can pick up the phone to call my mother or mother-in-law and say, "Help," and words of wisdom, experience, and reassurance are sure to follow.

I Want My Momma

Near the top of my least-favorite-things list is hearing Jessie cry. I remember wondering on our first night home from the hospital how something so small could make so much noise for such a long period of time. It was one of the few times when I was glad that I can't hear as well as I used to. Our poor dog, who has excellent hearing, couldn't take it; she left the room any time Jessie cried.

Kids "cry" and they "CRY." Parents can tell the difference in an instant.

After school yesterday, Jessie and I decided to take a bike ride around the neighborhood. Jessie put on her bike helmet, elbow pads, and kneepads. She started down the driveway on her bike and I followed on mine. I'm not sure what happened, but she wrecked her bike before she got out of the driveway. It didn't seem that serious, but out came the "CRY."

Unfortunately, when Jessie fell, the bike's handlebar hit her in the mouth. I saw her put her hand to her mouth and spit a tooth into it and her "CRY" turned into a "CRYYYYYYY!" Then I wanted to cry, too, as I would much rather spend my money on a new tennis racquet than dentist bills, but I tried to keep calm as I assessed the injury.

If crying is number two on my least-favorite list, then blood is number one. Fortunately, the tooth that Jessie knocked out was an already-loose baby tooth. However, both the empty tooth hole and a small cut on her lip were bleeding. My crying daughter, holding her tooth and dripping blood, requested a tissue. What a bad time for this experienced dad not to have a tissue in his pocket. Luckily, my mom raised me to carry a clean handkerchief each day. I quickly handed it to Jessie. We walked into the house with tears streaming down her cheeks and a bloodstained hanky stuffed in her mouth.

When Jessie calmed down, she said, "I want my momma." By now, I wanted her momma, too, along with my momma and my momma-in-law.

Jessie wanted her mom, not her Mr. Mom. I'm a great dad and Jessie knows both her father and mother will always love her unconditionally. However, there is a special bond between a mother and her child. We called Mattie at her office. As soon as Jessie finished talking with her momma, life was back to normal, except for her less-toothy smile. Then, Jessie and I went on our bike ride.

My conclusion is simple. Moms are important!

This morning, as I drove Jessie to school, she thanked me for my hanky. Dads are important, too. Now, how am I going to get my bloodstained handkerchief clean? I think I'll call and ask my momma.

I Still Need Mom

A story idea can hit me at any time or place. I could be playing with Jessie, taking a shower, or even sitting in church. Of course, it wouldn't be during the pastor's sermon as he is a gifted speaker. Not to mention, he reads many of my stories. I began to formulate this story while hugging the toilet.

I propped my back against the bathroom wall during a break from regurgitating. My mom came to mind. No, I'm not saying that my mom makes me sick. I pondered how many times Mom nursed me back to health. On my knees, hunched over the porcelain bowl, I had two main thoughts. First, "It's time to clean the toilet" and second, "I want my mom!"

As I sat by the toilet wishing my mom was there to take care of me, I had time to reflect. I remembered the time Jessie crashed her bike and lost a baby tooth when her mouth hit the handlebar. The blood from her cut lip and missing tooth was easy to stop. Her tears were not. Jessie cried over and over, "I want my momma!" At the time, I wanted her momma, too. But even though I had the situation, along with Jessie's tooth, calmly in hand, she insisted she needed Momma. There is something about a mother's love and comfort.

When Jessie was about 2 years old, I took her for a week-long visit with my parents. Since there was not an extra bed at their house, I slept in a sleeping bag on the floor. Around 2 a.m., I woke up and my lips felt numb. I got up and looked in the bathroom mirror and discovered my lips were swollen to twice their normal size. I looked like a clown! A spider or some kind of bug must have bitten me. What should I do?

I started to have an anxiety attack. Is this how I was going to go out – allergic reaction, breathing stops, followed by death – all from a bug bite? My dad used to volunteer on the ambulance crew at the local volunteer fire company. I thought about waking him up, but decided to call Mom instead. She didn't wake up until the fourth or fifth loud whisper of "Mom!" but then she groggily stepped out of bed, like she must have done hundreds of times with her four kids. I told her that I got bit by something and showed her my clown lips. My daughter was afraid of clowns at the time, and I joked with Mom that "Jessie will be scared to look at her father."

Mom sat up with me for an hour in the middle of the night. We laughed until we both had tears in our eyes. More important, my mom comforted me and was there for me yet again. She didn't care what time of day or night, how old I was, or that I even looked like a clown.

A few hours after my toilet bowl fling, my stomach began to settle. I asked Mattie what she thought would be good for me to eat, and hopefully keep down. She suggested my mother's homemade applesauce. My mom makes the best applesauce, peeling apples and cooking them with sugar, then pureeing them in the blender. Every batch is a lot of work, yet she sends me home with a cooler full of it each time I make the 700-mile trip to visit. While I ate her applesauce, I realized how lucky I am that my mom is still taking care of me.

Since I've been a stay-at-home dad for eight years now, I have a better understanding – a *much* better understanding – of how hard parents work for their children. I also realize my job as a dad will never end, because children never outgrow needing their parents.

Mom, thank you for all you did, and continue to do, for me. My normal-sized lips have formed a smile many times in my life because of you, especially when I eat your applesauce.

Lessons Learned

It's not easy being a parent. In fact, sometimes it's downright frustrating, like when you have to correct your child for the same behavior over and over. Will the lessons ever be learned? That's why it's so gratifying when you can see that you're getting through.

Recently, I came home after playing tennis and said, "Jessie, I did something tonight that took a lot of courage." She wanted to know the details. I told her that I stopped playing tennis because of the weather, even though I expected my tennis buddies to tease me. The thunder had been rumbling in the distance for about 15 minutes. Every now and then, a flash of lighting lit up the sky. The pending storm didn't deter any of the other 15 men who were playing. When I saw yet another streak of lightning, I had a flashback to my childhood. My little brother and I frequently played at the neighborhood ball diamond. We knew if we didn't get home at the first sign of rain, there would be a "Mommastorm" when we walked in the house.

After I finished holding serve to complete a game, I told the other players I was calling it a night. That sounded much better than saying, "I'm quitting because I'm scared of the weather." I asked one of the players, a farmer, if he felt it was still safe to play. He said, "You never know when a stray lightning bolt might occur." Still, the rest of the men stayed on the courts while I packed my gear and went home. I told Jessie that it took courage for me to stop even though the other men continued playing.

Mattie used my story to reinforce a lesson from earlier in the day. Jessie's first-grade teacher had given each student a paper doll and instructed the students to take the dolls home and decorate them to reflect their interests. Jessie put a lot of thought into her project. She even made a pink dress for her paper doll in the style of the pink dress she planned to wear for the presentation and glued photocopies of her tennis shoes to the doll's feet. She skipped into school carrying her doll in a bag to keep it secret, anxious for the presentation time when the students would describe their dolls.

After school, Jessie told us that no one noticed that she and her doll were identically dressed. She told Mattie none of the other kids had the idea of matching outfits, so she didn't say anything. She wished she had pointed it out in her presentation. Mattie talked with Jessie about how everyone is unique. "People just need to do their best, and then be proud of who they are and what they do instead of trying to be like everybody else," she said. Then she reassured Jessie that this was a good learning opportunity and that she would have more courage the next time.

During bedtime prayers that evening, Jessie said "Thank you for helping Daddy make the right decision."

A smile came to my face. Maybe she's getting more from our lessons than I think.

Mom, I still come in when it storms. Your lessons stuck.

The Right Ingredients

Jessie and I have made pancakes together since she was three years old. Now age nine, she still enjoys mixing the ingredients, pouring the batter into the skillet, and flipping them. She loves making pancakes almost as much as eating them. However, because she smothers her pancakes with creative combinations of powdered sugar, various kinds of syrup, whipped cream, and cinnamon sugar butter, eating them rates pretty highly.

One recent Sunday, Jessie said, "Let's make pancakes for breakfast." I responded, "I could eat pancakes," and went to retrieve the mix from the pantry.

"Uh oh, Jessie, the box is almost empty."

Jessie, undeterred, went to her friend, Google. Seconds later, Jessie announced that she found an excellent pancake recipe. She tried to sell it to me by saying, "It has all 5-star ratings and one 4-star rating." She began to call out the ingredients from her desk, located just off the kitchen. Boy, she really didn't want oatmeal and yogurt, her standard weekday breakfast.

When Jessie said, "baking powder," I thought I'd be making oatmeal, as I was confident we lacked this ingredient. But I checked the pantry to make sure. Jessie got up from her desk and helped with the search.

"I'm sure we have some, Dad."

"I don't think so, Jessie."

My pantry looked disorganized before Jessie's hunt, but now I know what disorganized looks like.

I concluded we were out of luck, but Jessie refused to give up. She checked the pantry another time. She even searched the refrigerator. As I prepared to make oatmeal, I decided to check the cabinet where I keep a few spices and spotted the baking powder. It turns out that Jessie was right and I was wrong. She was so excited when I pulled out the white can and held it in the air. I think it was because we could try her pancake recipe and not because she was right and I was wrong.

We gathered all the ingredients and prepared to make five-star pancakes from scratch. Jessie even felt comfortable tweaking the recipe. Instead of one tablespoon of sugar per the recipe, well, let's just say the batter contained adequate sugar. As she mixed all the ingredients, I pulled out the electric skillet. Jessie, with spatula in hand, then uttered the words we hear so frequently, "Don't look, please!" Jessie likes to surprise her mom and me with whatever she is doing (creating art, making a salad, etc.), and only wants us to see the finished product. So, I left her in charge and headed to the kitchen table to read the Sunday newspaper.

As Jessie poured the mixed batter into the skillet and joyfully flipped away, I couldn't help but peek up periodically from my paper. It seems like only yesterday I was standing over her 3-year-old shoulders to make sure she didn't burn herself on the hot skillet or fall off of the stool she needed to reach it. Six years zoomed by quicker than Jessie and I found baking powder.

As I reminisced, Jessie provided me with periodic updates. "They're thicker; they'll be more filling." "I burnt myself. I'm okay. It's only a third-degree burn." I noticed that she gave Sadie a few sample tastes. Jessie had a grand time making pancakes two at a time in a skillet that could have held eight. "I like dragging it out," she said.

Now that I've had time to reflect on this experience, I have learned a number of things. Don't rush to make microwaved oatmeal. Extra sugar makes pancakes sweeter. Have enough soap on hand for cleaning up after "not looking." A five-star breakfast is a great way to begin a Sunday, especially for a dog. In addition, the experience was a good reminder that Dad isn't always right.

I've also concluded that besides eggs, flour, salt, sugar, milk, and baking powder, one other ingredient is needed. Extra sugar? No. Vanilla? Different story.

It's patience. Patience to teach. Patience to learn. Patience to sit back and not run to the rescue. Spilled milk is easy to clean, although egg slime dripping down the kitchen cabinet takes some effort. Patience to listen. And patience to not say "no" right away. I'll also need patience to rearrange my messy pantry.

Before long, Jessie will be ready to try another recipe. I don't know if I'll have all the ingredients and in the right quantity. But, regardless of my pantry's status or my patience level, I'll never run out of the most important ingredient – love.

May your days, especially Mother's Day, be filled with an extra tablespoon of sugar as you fill your recipes and your homes with love.

Thank You ... at 70 words per minute

Thank you – two words, only eight letters. "Thanks" could cut it to a single word. Heck, sometimes words aren't even needed – a warm embrace, held hand, or gentle forehead kiss are effective nonverbal ways to show appreciation. Of course, it's even more special when "Thanks" is followed by "I love you."

Last July, I drove 15 hours to Pennsylvania for my mother's serious operation. It didn't seem that long since Mom combed my hair to get me ready for school. Luckily, since she drove the school bus (for 43 years), my chances of missing it were miniscule. Somehow those school days had long passed and now my tough, energetic mother was frail.

The words "stressed, fatigued, and worried" summed up my emotional week. I pondered the role reversal from my younger years as I brushed Mom's hair and fed her ice chips, broth, and Jell-O. Mom just peeled and cut bananas for my morning cereal. Now I had to excite her about the tray of clear liquids delivered to her hospital room. All the times she held a tissue to my nose and said, "Blow," pinching – in my opinion – too hard, came to mind when I became the holder of the tissue and issued the command.

The "Fall Risk" sign posted outside her hospital room took me back to the days when I held my outstretched arms for Jessie to prevent my toddler from falling. Now my ailing mom needed the assistance. How did the years go so fast?

One day, after Mom had finished her unappetizing lunch, I headed to the hospital cafeteria. As I walked down the hallway, I saw an elderly man with a cane who looked familiar. I stopped and hesitantly asked, "Mr. Fuhrman?"

"Yes."

"I thought that was you. You haven't changed a bit. Patrick Hempfing, class of 1978. I had you for typing in high school."

After I exchanged pleasantries with the teacher I hadn't seen for 36 years, I asked, "Guess what I do for a living?" Before he could answer I blurted out, "I'm a writer. I can still type 70 words a minute." To be honest, this may have been a slight overstatement, though I am proficient with the keyboard.

I filled Mr. Fuhrman in on all the jobs I've performed since I took his class. He smiled when I told him that, a few weeks earlier, I thought about him when I instructed Jessie to "place her fingers on the home row keys." I've been trying to teach her to type instead of peck. As our meeting concluded, I thanked him for making a difference in my life. I'm not sure which of us enjoyed our chance meeting in the hospital more, but I know we both cherished the moment.

Months have passed since that week-long visit to the hospital, and I am thankful that Mom is doing better. She turned 80 in November and is as feisty as ever. After her hospital stint, she spent three weeks in rehab. Much to her dismay, she had to re-take her driver's test before she could drive again. She set a goal, took the test, and passed. Thank you, Mom, for the great lesson on perseverance.

Jessie, the next time you're faced with a challenge and feel like saying, "I can't," think of your Mom Maw and her driver's test. You can do it. I also want you to always keep a thankful heart and express your gratitude with warm hugs and kind words, spoken, written in cursive, or typed, regardless of how fast you can press the keys. We can't all have Mr. Fuhrman as our typing teacher.

Spoken Words

"It's not easy being a parent. In fact, sometimes it's downright frustrating, like when you have to correct your child for the same behavior over and over."

These were the opening sentences for the first Mother's Day column I wrote. It's been three years and I still feel the same. Of course, there are two sides to every story. It's not easy being a child, either. In fact, sometimes it's downright frustrating, like when your parents continue to nag you over and over.

I'm sure all parents have given the "think before you speak" speech. Jessie has heard this speech a few times, with a special emphasis on "It's not just what you say, but how you say it."

But, whether you're a kid or an adult, we've all been there, wishing we could take back words or deliver them over with a different tone.

Prior to a recent corrective-action discussion (Jessie calls them lectures), I had a flashback to my sixth-grade days. I hadn't thought about this story in years — maybe I blocked it out. But it's a perfect story of a 12-year-old boy not learning the "think before you speak" rule. After this experience, though, I had a much firmer grasp of the concept.

Near the end of our school day, we were supposed to be working. However, the second-grade class played dodge ball in the courtyard outside our window. The teacher, Mrs. Dowd, instructed us to focus on our work, not the second graders. I'm not sure what the teacher said next, but smart-alecky me, trying to get a laugh, raised my hand and said, "I'll go out and play with them." Needless to say, my response didn't sit well with Mrs. Dowd. She gave me two choices, march down to the principal's office or head outside to play with the second graders. Since playing sounded much better than bending over and grabbing my ankles, as principals spanked during my school years, I chose dodge ball. I won't forget my embarrassment when I had to explain to the second-grade teacher why I crashed her students' game of dodge ball.

When second-grade recess ended, I walked back into my classroom. Had I learned my lesson? I'm sure I was trying to save face with my classmates when I told my teacher, "That was fun. I'd do that again." I've never won an award for being a quick learner, but I did realize at that point I had just forced Mrs. Dowd to intensify my training.

"Okay then. The next time we have recess, you can stay in to work and then go out with the second-grade class for their recess." By that point in time, the light bulb in my brain flickered with the notion that maybe I should keep my smart mouth shut.

It's good this happened near the end of the school day, because my stomach felt like it had taken a direct hit from a dodge ball. Somehow, though, I kept it together until I made it home. Then I cried. During supper that evening, more tears flowed as I told my parents what happened and begged them to, "Please talk to my teacher so she doesn't make me play with the second graders again." Of course, in my heart I knew my parents would never try to get me out of a punishment I richly deserved (and they didn't).

Luckily for me, Mrs. Dowd never followed through on her plan, and I gained a valuable lesson on the line between humor and disrespect. It seems obvious, but we all have to learn the importance of the timing, tone, and content of our words, and that sometimes silence is golden. I try to share this with Jessie to spare her the pain of learning it the hard way like I did.

Jessie is likely in for more lectures in the tween and teen years ahead. I'll try to deliver them without nagging, but I'm likely to fail. Remember, I'm not a quick learner. As often as I can, though, I'll share my own childhood experiences so she'll know I was once in her shoes. I hope she'll listen to my carefully spoken words.

Thanks to the parents who teach their children all kinds of lessons, sometimes repeatedly. May all of us remember to conclude our corrective-action discussions with three important words that apply to every lecture topic, "I love you."

Chapter 8

A Strong Finish

Hodgepodge – The daily life of a parent is filled with a mixed bag of anything and everything. Parents perform a wide variety of tasks in their 24/7 schedule and experience different emotions and demands, some of which test their skills and endurance. There are the great "I don't want this moment to end" times, but also "Okay, count to 10 and stay patient" moments. Parenthood accentuates the joys and tribulations of life, with all of its highs and lows.

Luckily, I'm blessed with a strong support system, including my faith and work ethic. I try to keep a positive attitude and a good sense of humor. Does my attitude always stay positive? No. Am I always laughing? Of course not. Are there days I feel like collapsing on the sofa at 10 a.m.? Power naps are my friends. With that said, parenting is a job like no other. We can't say, "I'm checking out for the day" or "I'm taking Tuesday off." No, we need to roll up our sleeves and finish strong, or at least finish, because others depend on us.

This chapter is the strong finish to my book, with a hodgepodge of stories that reflect the many hats I wear as husband, father, son, sibling, and author. Six of them won awards in writing contests that had specific criteria. For example, *Jesus and Momma* won first place for writing that exemplifies the Southern spirit ... not a bad achievement for a man who lived in Pennsylvania until he was 36. *Wife or Dog* was the winning entry for a true story about the writer's best friend. *Celebrate*, the last story in the book, won a contest for a true story about a supportive sibling. It is a poignant reminder of why we need to celebrate every day and cherish the moments.

The Secret

I found it! Jessie showed me. Why didn't I find it sooner? The important thing is that I found it. The "it" is the secret to making a young girl giddy with happiness — not just cheery, but full-fledged, cup-overflowing jubilant. If you have a son, bear with me, as I'll bring in the boys later.

Jessie has been at home with me, rather than in school, the past week because of spring break. Her mom, Mattie, had to work. I had a full week of work, too. Jessie's class is beginning to learn multiplication. I teased her that over her spring break, Jessie would be attending the "Patrick L. Hempfing Home School of Math." It's safe to say Jessie wouldn't declare multiplication tables to be the secret to happiness. However, my week's lesson plan called for me to mix in a little math with other exciting activities. As it turned out, the time spent on fun activities far outweighed the time spent practicing 7 x 7.

The weekend started with an art festival. Prior to visiting the art stands, Jessie's ballet class performed on the community stage. Mattie snapped photos and I took video footage of our ballerina's first public performance. After the show, Mattie and Jessie shared a bag of cotton candy, and we visited the first art table. Then, Mattie went home, as it's not her thing to visit every crowded stand to watch Jessie paint, color, mold clay, make bracelets, tap instruments, and whatever else. Jessie and I had a wonderful daddy-daughter date as we visited *all* the stands. I found out, though, that going home covered in paint and dry clay with sticky fingers from eating cotton candy and drinking frozen lemonade is not the secret to a girl's intensely joyful state, although it's a pretty effective path to a tired dad.

Many other events took place during spring break week. I made a pot of hard-boiled eggs. Of course, Jessie wanted to help peel them – by the light of our battery-operated lantern to make it more fun. Not the secret, though 2 ruined eggs times 2 ruined eggs equals 4. Jessie helped me dry dishes. She ate a few peanut butter and jelly sandwiches. We made a delicious pot of macaroni and cheese that had to set a record for the amount of cheese one child can put into a pot. Maybe we should have practiced fractions instead of multiplication tables.

"Jessie, you can only use ¼ of the block of Velveeta cheese."

Did I mention these activities occurred while listening to music from Taylor Swift? Somehow, the "Patrick L. Hempfing School of Math" turned into the "Jessie Hempfing School of Music" with Jessie teaching me the words to all of Taylor Swift's songs. Still, I hadn't found the secret.

I took Jessie to the park and tennis courts a few days. As much as I'd like to say the secret to giddy happiness is playing tennis with Dad, unfortunately, I cannot. Jessie did enjoy riding her scooter around the park's track until she fell and skinned her knee. Having Dad's clean handkerchief wrapped around a bloody knee is not the secret. Jessie enjoyed roller skating on a different day. Though it didn't involve any bleeding, it didn't prove to be the secret.

One day, we took Jessie's friend to the park. When her friend said, "Last one to the picnic table is a rotten egg," I didn't realize it included me. Okay, so two 8-year-old girls are faster than a middle-aged man with a torn medial meniscus who didn't realize he was part of the race. By this point in time, it's safe to say I felt closer to 62 than 22, but fortunately, footraces with Dad are not the secret.

Mattie has taken Jessie to yoga classes a few times. One day, Jessie said she'd be better prepared for her multiplication tables if we did yoga first. So we listened to Taylor (I'm on a first name basis now) as yoga instructor Jessie took charge. She did fess up that everything she attempted to have me do might not be considered yoga, but, she explained "It's good for you." Let's just say I used my torn medial meniscus as an excuse several times. There were right splits, left splits, and middle splits. Then Jessie described something called a "butterfly," where I needed to "pinch my nose between my toes." This involved sitting with the bottoms of my feet touching and my knees bent out to the sides, then bending forward from the waist until my nose touched the floor.

"Jessie, can we go back to learning more of Taylor's songs?" I reached the conclusion that my body was in better shape back in my Barry Manilow days.

I nailed two men's push-ups (all she asked me to do). Thank goodness she didn't say do 4 x 5 push-ups. She must have questioned my fitness level, though, because she said, "If you can't do 2 men's push-ups, try 5 girls' push-ups instead."

Though Jessie enjoyed her yoga class, this still is not the secret, nor is getting an ice pack from the freezer to put on Dad's sore knee afterwards.

Jessie did many other activities during her spring break week. She had fun digging holes in the yard and planting flower seeds. I should have had her dig 4 holes on each side of the sidewalk to hammer home 4 x 2, but I missed that teachable moment. She had fun husking corn and intentionally spreading corn silk over her shirt and pants so I could vacuum them off of her. It made for a few giggles, but not the secret to exuberant happiness.

I let her push the lawn mower out of the garage, without the engine running so it would be safe, as she wanted to help me mow the lawn. As I mowed, Jessie sat on the porch with a pencil, pad, and tambourine, and wrote a song. I imagine Taylor Swift did the same in her youth.

Who knows, maybe she even followed her dad while playing the tambourine and singing her newly written song as he tried to mow, not unlike Jessie. Though this had to be my most entertaining mowing experience ever, it still wasn't the secret. Jessie also enjoyed spraying water on my face to keep me cool while I mowed, but that's no secret.

She made her bed. Not the secret. She sat in the church pew. That's not it either. She knocked the modem off the corner of my desk, temporarily knocking out my internet service. That, for sure, wasn't the secret to my happiness. Jessie also enjoyed eating cherry dessert pizza at Pizza Hut, making a pizza from scratch with her friend and her friend's dad, and doing her spelling homework. Okay, I threw in the spelling homework. It's probably time I reveal the secret, as spelling homework is worse than multiplication tables.

A few days before Jessie performed in her first ballet, the teacher handed out tutus to all the girls. I never witnessed anything like it. I saw apparently normal girls turn giddy. The tutu appeared to give Jessie magical powers. She could leap higher. She had increased flexibility. Her spins were faster. But her smile stole my heart. As I watched my girl perform in her tutu, my eyes welled.

So I've concluded that a tutu is the secret to a girl's special kind of happiness, at least for my 8-year-old daughter. Though it's likely that all the quality time spent with Mom and Dad (she'd argue that spelling homework and multiplication tables don't count) is also mighty important.

As for parents with sons, while a tutu isn't likely going to be the secret for them, here's my take. Little girls in tutus grow up to be lovely young ladies. Little boys grow into young men. Young man meets young lady. Voilà, love and happiness go together.

For now, though, I'm going to enjoy the tutu years. Before long, I'll be buying her pointe shoes. Will they have the same effect as a tutu? When Jessie tries them on, will she instantly grow 3 feet and be looking down at her 6'5" father? Only time will tell what one tutu plus one pair of pointe shoes will equal. But whether I'm looking up at my tall, beautiful girl on pointe or down to the little one in a tutu, Jessie will know I love her, and that's no secret.

The Nine-Fingered Writer

Albert Einstein, Isaac Newton, Leonardo da Vinci, and me? My name used in the same breath as these great minds is unlikely. To be honest, I'm not sure whether I'd make it on my wife's Top-100 list of reasonably smart acquaintances. If I ever was there, I may have dropped off when I tried to squeeze too much out of my day before leaving for a family vacation last summer.

I mowed grass, did the laundry, made supper, and washed the dishes, just another normal day. When I finished the supper dishes, I mowed for one more hour with the mosquitos keeping me company. As I put the mower in the garage, the sun had already gone to bed. I should have followed the sun's lead, but I didn't. I grabbed my hand clippers, not even taking time to put on my work gloves, as I wanted to trim two bushes beside the house. I trimmed the first bush, no problem. Then it happened. My hand clippers introduced themselves to the middle finger on my left hand. "Ouch!" To put it more strongly, "OUCH!"

I ran into the house – fast. The blood flowed freely from the end of my sliced finger. I won't even mention the pain. I'll vouch, though, that fingertips contain more nerve endings than other parts of the body. Mine were screaming "idiot" at me. A drop of blood landed above my right knee and dripped down to the top of my white sock. I calmly announced my presence; okay, "calmly"

201

probably isn't the right adverb. What was I to say when Mattie came running? "Hey, your intelligent husband trimmed bushes in the dark and cut off his finger." I lost both pride and blood with one little snip.

Mattie bandaged my finger. She didn't have a bandage big enough for my wounded pride. So I did what any man in my position would do. I took my injured finger, wrapped a sheet of paper towel, two-ply, around the bandage for extra protection, and went back outside to finish the job. I picked up the hand clippers that I had hastily thrown in the grass minutes earlier. Then, under moonlit sky, I carefully snipped the remaining branches with my healthy right hand. This time, however, I let the branches fall to the ground rather than attempting to grab them with my now-injured left hand. Job done.

Even before this event, I realized the importance of good common sense. Indeed, it's safer to cut things when one can clearly see what they're lopping off. I cringe to think what could have happened if I had tried this while gardening at a nudist colony and missed my cut by a few inches in the other direction. I would have called Mattie's name with a much higher pitch and an even greater sense of urgency. Then for sure, I'd be off her list, and she'd never again let me carve our holiday turkeys. Give me some credit; at least I used the hand clippers instead of pulling out my electric hedge trimmers.

From my youth, I've always taken pride in being a hard worker with a good attitude. If a person puts in the hours and maintains a positive attitude, good things will happen, right? As Mattie bandaged my finger, I can't say I felt love and appreciation for all my sweat and blood. Instead of earning a badge of honor, I sensed she'd gladly stick a bandage of stupidity to my chest (maybe even if I wasn't wearing a shirt).

So what did I learn that evening? I'll be the first to admit my priorities were off that ill-conceived night. I should have left a few straggly branches for another time. Apparently, Mattie is attracted to intelligent people and isn't at all impressed with valiant acts of stupidity. I also learned a writer needs 10 healthy fingers. I type a lot of words that contain the letters, e, d, and c (letters typed by my left middle finger).

Without this finger, chores I type on my To-Do list might never get done, such as "wash th ar," "pik up th launry," and "tak th og to th vt." I'd also have a tough time romancing Mattie with typed love notes. What's my valentine to think when she finds a note stuck to the bathroom mirror that reads, "Mt m unr th tr in th bakyar for a romanti pini at noon." My guess is I would end up eating too much when I found myself sitting alone with my picnic lunch for two.

As for my writing career, well, I can't think of any prominent nine-fingered writers. Would the beginning of this query letter hook a book publisher? "Dar itor, I'm th writr for you. I may b short a fingr, but I mak up for it with my crativity." With this opening, I won't need to run to the mailbox to look for an advance check, no matter how creative I am.

Mark Twain, Ernest Hemingway, Charles Dickens, and me? Will my name join this elite group of writers? It's unlikely. But, by using good common sense and working hard, I hope to promote my books across the country one day. Of course, I need to maintain a good attitude, too. I can't say I had the best of attitudes the next morning when I got my tetanus shot. Apparently, I didn't make the nurse's list of smartest patients, either, but hey, at least I didn't have to drop my drawers, as my arm took the hit. More important, I still had ten fingers, nine working, and one ready for vacation.

Hormone Collision

We've all heard the expression, "Timing is everything." Due to anticipated timing in my household, I have a feeling I'll need to incorporate a new motto within the next few years – "Square footage is everything."

My residence is already too small, even though it only houses a slightly spoiled 9-year-old daughter; a sweet, intelligent, wonderful, loving, devoted, drop-dead gorgeous wife; a 22-pound Shetland sheepdog; and a peacemaking stay-at-home dad. If I write a menopause story about Mattie, whose next birthday will be her first that begins with a five, I'd better use a lot of glowing adjectives to describe her.

Prior to Jessie's arrival, my wife and I had focused on our careers and education. Mattie gave birth to Jessie at age 39, 19 years after she became my bride. Five years Mattie's senior, I accepted new responsibilities as a stay-at-home dad. The baby years involved lots of diapers, but I survived. The toddler years required lots of steps, but I kept pace. Recent years have entailed lots of words, but I've filtered through the 100,000 extra ones Jessie speaks each day.

However, in a few years, something tells me I'm in for a heap of trouble as Mattie and Jessie are on a collision course – menopause and puberty. Mattie and Jessie both have Type-A personalities. They are natural-born Alpha dogs, great at taking charge and directing activities, achieving their goals by persuasion or tenacity. Neither is patient or likes to take direction. You might say they each like to be in control. What will this Type-B stay-at-home dad do? Well, let's just say I plan to buy a new cushion for my "man chair," tucked in the corner of the garage.

According to WebMD, the symptoms of menopause "may include hot flashes, night sweats, pain during intercourse, increased anxiety or irritability, and the need to urinate more often." I'm hoping the facial hair it says she could grow won't make her look as goofy as I do with a mustache, or as menacing as I did the time I grew a beard.

Then there's Jessie, three months away from her 10th birthday. I so enjoyed the easy days when I only had to pick up Cheerios that Jessie had thrown from her high chair or change a T-shirt covered with spittle, vomit, or anything else that came from one of her orifices. One day, though, I know I'll need to make a trip to Walmart, down the aisle across from the pharmacy, to purchase a box of … did I mention I need a new seat cushion for my man chair? That's what I'll do; I'll go to Walmart and shop for a new seat cushion, while Jessie goes to pick up that blue and white box filled with 36 or 48 or whatever quantity those "things" come in. Forget the "light days" and "heavy days." I'm thinking, "man chair days!"

Okay, so I know what lies waiting in my future. There will be one female who wishes this period would not have started and another female sad this period has ended, though I doubt any woman actually looks forward to, dare I say it, menstruation.

I barely made it through Sadie's first, and only, heat, which unfortunately came early. I had my calendar marked for the beginning of the following month, "Take Sadie to get fixed." Two weeks too early, however, I found spots of blood on the floor, and noticed Sadie had developed a strange attraction to Jessie's 2-foot-tall stuffed penguin.

Jessie called Mattie, who was, far too conveniently in my estimation, away at a conference.

"Sadie has her period," she informed her mom.

Then, to help relieve her concern and stress, she wrote notes to her grandmothers and other female family members to notify them of the worrisome circumstances. I made a call to a different woman, one well equipped to help me with this delicate situation – the vet. Unfortunately, I doubt she'll be able to similarly prevent Mattie or Jessie from acting weird.

That's when my man chair will be there to support me. At some point, however, I'll need to bravely leave it. Then, I'll need a strategic plan to elude the personalities involved in what could escalate into a war of body changes. Though my plan is still under development, I have a few tactics already in place. I plan to beat my tennis buddies an extra set or two on tennis nights. Tennis outings might go from two to possibly seven nights a week. In addition to the extra time away, the exercise will build my immune system. I'm pretty sure there will be some things to which I'll need to become immune.

I'll slowly push mow my lawn and pull every single weed. I might even be a good neighbor and pluck the weeds from my neighbor's yard. Jessie has always wanted a flower garden. This will require trips to the store for supplies and hours of outdoor labor. Heck, when I'm done with the flower garden, maybe I'll plant a vegetable garden, too. Like exercise, fresh vegetables are good for the immune system. One can't have too many trees either, even though it will take longer to mow around them.

After the yard and garden are completed, it will be time to wash the vehicles. I plan a weekly washing, at a minimum. Depending how Mattie and Jessie are cohabitating inside, I might have the cleanest cars in the neighborhood in a few years, even though both vehicles are in bad shape at the moment.

As a loving spouse and father, I'll be sure to peek in the house window to make sure all is well with my two Alpha loved ones. I'll probably notice the windows are dirty and may choose to wash them even if they aren't. I'm pretty sure I'll be taking Sadie for lots of walks, too. She's been just fine since her "procedure," but I wouldn't want her to put on weight. I can hear the neighbors talking already. "Wow, that Patrick has the cleanest car and healthiest dog in the neighborhood."

But, after all that hard work, it will be nice to finish my day by curling up with Mattie. I'll snuggle up next to her in bed and put my arm around her. What are the chances I'll hear, "Get away from me. I'm hot!" Thank goodness my strategic plan includes a "man sofa," as I can't sleep comfortably in my man chair.

As I lie on the sofa, looking up at the living room ceiling, I'll remain patient and strong, knowing that Mattie will make it through her hot flashes, night sweats, and increased need to urinate. Heck, I haven't made it through a night without having to get up to pee in 10 years, so if I can handle it, Mattie can, too.

Who knows, maybe my worries are unfounded and the menopause/puberty collision won't occur. Could it even be a blessing? For example, one recent evening as I typed at my desk in the dining room, Jessie called out from her bedroom, "I'm hot." I turned the thermostat down a couple of degrees and went back to work. Fifteen minutes couldn't have passed when Mattie yelled from the master bedroom on the opposite side of the house, "I'm cold." My forehead dropped onto my keyboard. One hot, one cold, and one caught in the middle. Instead of running to my man chair, I bravely turned the thermostat up a degree. Fortunately, Jessie had fallen asleep so she didn't complain.

Luckily, if Mattie does begin to have hot flashes, I'll be fine since Jessie likes cooler temperatures. I'll simply turn the thermostat down and both my girls will be happy. Maybe while I'm shopping for my seat cushion at Walmart, I'll buy myself a sweater.

Still, this little voice in my head tells me I'll need more than a man chair, a man sofa, and a new sweater to make it through the next several years. I think when menopause and puberty overlap for Mattie and Jessie, this man will need a bigger place to live – and hide. Maybe I'll find a house with a detached building I could turn into a man cave. But, whether I do or not, the key will be square footage because size matters – especially when female hormones are involved, as I've read they tend to make all kinds of things grow.

Being There

Swoosh! Jessie banked a 10-footer off the backboard, her third basket of the game, helping to propel her team to victory in the intramural basketball championship game. Each time she scored, her proud dad wanted the refs to blow the whistle to stop the game for a celebration. I wished I could run onto the court, lift her high in the air and say to the crowd "Did you see that? That was my girl!" My guess is that most fans already knew she was my daughter due to my extra loud cheers in the stands. But the main thing was that Jessie knew I saw her big plays. I was there.

I enjoy sports, whether I'm a participant or spectator. Growing up, my family's financial resources were limited, but we had enough money for basketballs, footballs, baseballs, and gloves. A ball diamond was a short bike ride away. Many of my best childhood memories occurred on the baseball field with my brothers and friends. I played third base in little league and spent my evenings watching Brooks Robinson, third baseman for the Baltimore Orioles, on our black and white TV. I loved playing the "hot corner." I would dive at balls like Brooks did, even if they were already past me into left field. Boys like to get dirty. I would come running in on bunts to pick up the slow moving ball with my bare hand and throw off-balance to first base. Unlike Brooks, my throws were often off-target.

It's been more than 40 years since my first start at third base. I've played many other positions. I've also played professionally, but in banking, accounting, and auditing, not baseball. My best position, however, has been as a father.

My dad, a self-employed mechanic for 47 years, worked six days a week from morning until night. While my father worked in the garage, my mother raised four kids and, for 43 years, drove a school bus. They both worked very hard, but when Sunday morning came, I knew we would be in the church pew.

My father didn't take an interest in sports. Many times I heard him say, "They can play the game without you." That comment always irritated me. I thought he just didn't understand. I can recall only two times when my parents came to watch me play. All kids want their parents to see them in action and to hear, "I'm proud of you." However, I realized they had many pressing responsibilities, so I dealt with it. But I didn't want to hear, "They can play the game without you."

Luckily, my brother Phil, who was nine years older than me, taught my younger brother and me to play baseball, football, and basketball. I gained my passion for sports from him.

At our church, sixth graders attended confirmation classes. Normally, these were not held on Saturday mornings, which in my week were reserved for little league baseball. However, for some reason, the pastor decided to schedule a class one Saturday. If sixth-grade boys were surveyed about whether they would rather be playing baseball or sitting in church, I'm confident that playing baseball would win in a landslide. I would definitely have picked baseball.

Although I could have argued with my religious father to let me skip the confirmation class, it would have been pointless. I knew he would just say, "They can play the game without you."

Needless to say, I didn't have a good attitude when Saturday morning arrived. I don't remember too much about that morning's confirmation class. I think we were quizzed on naming the books of the Bible and being able to recite the Apostles' Creed.

When confirmation class ended, I rushed to the baseball field, hoping to play for part of the game. My team, trailing by six or seven runs, didn't even field a full team, as only eight players had shown up. My dad was right; they could play the game without me. The coach immediately inserted me into the lineup at second base.

I hoped to play like Brooks Robinson someday, but at 12, I was a better fielder than hitter. I struck out my fair share of times and didn't hit home runs.

The first time I came to bat that day, I hit a single, knocking in two runs. Our team smelled a comeback. The bases were loaded for my second at-bat. I hit a shot between the center and right fielders and ran like crazy. I emptied the bases for a grand slam home run. I had one final at-bat and hit a solo home run, my second of the day. Our team came all the way back to win the game. My line score read three hits in three plate appearances with seven runs batted in (RBIs), an offensive explosion from a boy better known for his defensive abilities.

The coach took our whole team down to my father's garage for celebratory sodas. Dad was in the garage working, as usual. He could tell that our team won. My coach told him how great I did. I felt like a hero. I told several teammates that I should go to church every Saturday.

Did God reward me for going to confirmation class instead of the baseball game? Could it have been divine intervention? I don't know. I do know that my parents laid the groundwork for my faith by taking me to church every Sunday. But the day that my faith grew stronger was that Saturday morning. I believe there was a greater power at work than the muscles of a 12-year-old boy.

A lot has happened in my life since then. In my early 20s, I played church softball. My girlfriend often came to watch. She became my wife and, after 19 years of marriage, we were blessed with a beautiful daughter. I'm playing catch with her these days. She wears a pink ball glove as we toss balls onto the roof of our house and race to see who can catch them when they fall. Fatherhood is the greatest!

Of course, life also has its sorrows. My older brother, the one who stuck a ball in my hand, died way too young from cancer. Fifteen years later, cancer took my father to join him in heaven. I think about my dad every day, and am thankful that he left me with the greatest gift a father can give, a faith in God. Dad knew he wouldn't always be around for me, but God would.

One of my favorite things to do these days is take my daughter to sporting events. Although I've been to many exciting games, the most memorable was a local baseball game that Jessie and I watched together. Jessie got cold, so I held her on my lap and wrapped my jacket around her. Home runs by the home team pale in comparison to holding my little girl.

After her recent elementary basketball championship game, I walked onto the court as Jessie ran toward me. I picked her up and gave her the biggest hug while I told her how proud I was of her. It didn't matter how many baskets were scored, rebounds grabbed, or assists dished out. Though it was nice that her team scored more points than the opposing team, that was of minor importance, too. I was there and that's what truly mattered, to both of us.

This past Easter Sunday, I sat in church with Mattie and Jessie. As the opening hymn began, my eyes welled up and I started to sob. I could hear my father's voice singing with me, like he had done on most of the Easter Sundays of my life. It's been over three years since he died, yet I couldn't sing the first two verses while I struggled to regain my composure. I thought how my dad would be proud of me for the job I'm doing with my family. I know he would be happy to see his granddaughter in the church pew each Sunday.

Dad was right that they could play the game without me. He was right in prioritizing church over baseball. I'm fortunate I have more time to spend with my child than my father had with his children. As I sit in the stands watching Jessie play, or kneel beside her bed for evening prayers, I feel lucky to be able to pass on the important lessons I learned from my dad and brother. Sometimes it's as simple as being there. But when I'm not, I know that God is.

Jesus and Momma

"Y'all ready to start?" I asked this question on a Pennsylvania tennis court a few years ago as I prepared to play my sister and her boyfriend. My sister quickly responded, "Y'all!" as if I'd just said a bad four-letter word. "Y'all" is now a standard pronoun in my vocabulary as this former Yankee has spent the past 17 years in God's country ... the South.

Now I must confess I didn't always view the South this way. I should also add I can be quite stubborn and don't always keep an open mind. I was born in Pennsylvania, only a few miles north of the Mason-Dixon line. I shoveled snow for 36 years and in all likelihood would still be shoveling if it wasn't for a beautiful southern belle who lived 10 short minutes away, south of the border, down in Maryland. She had family all over the South – North Carolina, Tennessee, and Florida.

We met at a church located two miles north of the Maryland line. Three years later, we were married in the same church. Even before saying, "I do," I knew what my new bride's response would have been if I asked whether she wanted to spend her life in Pennsylvania. "I don't." So after 11 years of marital bliss in my home state, we gave away our snow shovels, packed our possessions, and headed to Florida, Mattie's dream state. One of us was ecstatic; the other, not so much. Another person who was less than thrilled was my mom.

However, a man must live his life, so I entered the Sunshine State with the song "Jesus and Mama" on my mind. The song, recorded by Confederate Railroad, is about a man reflecting on the two people who always loved him – no matter what he did. My momma was mad at me, really mad, but I knew she still loved me.

Now, I can't say I immediately fell in love with the South. I suffered a major bout of homesickness. To ease the loneliness, I made frequent visits to the donut shop for comfort food. On more than one occasion as I sat alone in our apartment, I had to remind myself that Jesus and Momma still loved me.

On January 1, 1997, five months removed from Pennsylvania, I took pictures by the apartment pool to send home to my family and friends, who were shoveling snow up north. Was it possible that short winter visit to the pool awakened me to some of the benefits of southern living? Gainesville is a great city and the residents love their Gator football, which was contagious even to a Penn State fan. My trips to the donut shop became less frequent. Mattie and I enjoyed sun-soaked walks while our Northern friends were staying indoors or had to bundle themselves in parkas to go outside. I had to admit it was more fun to swing a tennis racquet than a snow shovel. I also noticed that people in Gainesville welcomed us into their homes with the warm southern hospitality I'd heard about.

After five happy years in Gainesville, I followed my wife's career to South Carolina. I remember Mattie crying as we drove out of Florida. I didn't cry, but was truly sad to leave the city that had become my home. Interestingly, I didn't need to search for the nearest donut shop for comfort in South Carolina. We quickly met wonderful people who became our friends for life. I also learned about fatback. Didn't eat it, just learned what it was.

After six wonderful years in South Carolina, I again moved to support Mattie's career, this time to Georgia. Jesus and Momma still loved me as my wife, 2-year-old daughter, and I began the next southern chapter in our lives. It's hard to believe we've already lived six years here in the "gnat belt of the South," where the fields are filled with cotton and peanuts. Without a doubt, Statesboro has been the hottest place I've ever called home. It didn't surprise me, though, to find friendly folk here in the low country.

As I compare northern living with my life in the South, I've noticed a few differences, some obvious, others subtle. If I had to choose one word to sum up the differences, it would be "passion."

Now don't get me wrong, I know many wonderful and passionate people in Pennsylvania. However, I've noticed the passion over and over again here in the South. I've seen or felt it in residents' hugs, cooking, religion, football, and language. It took me a while to get used to all the greeting and departure hugs. Prior to moving south, I wasn't much of a hugger.

Though I haven't acquired a taste for grits and can't say okra is high on my favorite-foods list, I've tasted some of the best sausage and biscuit gravy ever made. I joke with Mattie that I sometimes wish I had married her Uncle Larry. His meals ooze passion for cooking. Our pastor stirs us with motivating sermons that make me want to come back Sunday after Sunday. Southerners love their football, too – Gators, Gamecocks, Tigers, Dawgs, and Eagles.

Language can be verbal, "Y'all come back any chance you get" or nonverbal. One recent evening, a number of cars in our neighborhood were broken into. The next afternoon, one of the neighbors took his elderly mother for a walk. He was toting his shotgun. Surprising, but passionate.

I'm not sure where else my life will lead. For now, I enjoy living in the land of cotton, even with its intense heat and gnats. It's a land where God shines down lots of sun on the friendly, passionate residents. It's where I call home. My mother, still up in Pennsylvania, doesn't like that very much. She wants me to move back. I don't worry about that, though, because I know that even when they wish I'd do things differently, Jesus and Momma love me.

Dog...Gone!

Tall? Check; I'm 6'5". Dark? Some gray, but most of my hair is still brown and present. Handsome? Okay, I'm not George Clooney, but babies don't cry when I walk by. Sometimes, though, I think I'd be better off being a fuzzy hairball with a cute bark. Mattie loves dogs. For six hours every February, she's glued to the TV watching the Westminster Kennel Club Dog Show. In fact, as I'm typing this, she's watching this year's competition with Jessie. For the past hour, all I've heard is "oh, so cute," "I want that one," and more "oohs" and "aahs" than I've gotten in 27 years of marriage. George Clooney could streak by right now and I doubt Mattie would even notice.

Mattie just called me in to see the border collie. She wants one. She also wants a bichon frise, bearded collie, and several others. Did I mention I just bought her a Shetland sheepdog? In fact, Mattie and Jessie are arguing over who gets to hold the 4-month-old puppy while they watch the dog show. Doggone, what's a husband to do?

I know one thing this husband must *not* do is lose the dog. Guess what I've done, not once or twice, but three times? Okay, the third time I had the dog in view, but I couldn't catch her, so technically I only lost control.

There are four things I hope never to say to my wife.

"Honey, we're out of toilet paper."

"I thought *you* put gas in the car."

The more serious, "It was only once, and she didn't mean anything to me."

The worst, "Honey, I lost the dog."

It wouldn't really matter which one of the last two I said because either way, she'd shoot me dead. The only difference would be that if I confessed to an affair, Mattie might ask a few questions before shooting. If I lost the dog, she'd pull the trigger faster than Jessie can turn a cartwheel.

I must agree that a competent man shouldn't lose an 8-year-old, 25-pound Shetland sheepdog … on a leash. So, I guess that Mattie didn't choose me as her lifelong mate for my brains. Doggone.

One cold morning a few years ago, I thought I was holding Ginger's leash, but it turned out I was only walking a bag of poop.

"But Mattie, I had on gloves and couldn't feel the leash."

"I was thinking about my manuscript that's going to make you millions."

"Don't shoot!"

Thank goodness, our obedience-school star was still standing where I dropped the leash to pick up after her. As relief replaced the panic on my face, Ginger's nonverbal communication said "Idiot!" Doggone, I don't get any respect.

Sadie, our eleven-week-old puppy, was the second Shetland sheepdog I lost. This wasn't my fault, but, as with most things around this household, "the blame stops here."

Apparently, the banging sounds that Jessie and her friend made on the front porch scared Sadie, who was inside. Though Sadie should have been easy to find because Jessie had dressed her in a brightly colored swimsuit, it took 10 minutes of frantic searching before we found her hiding in the laundry basket. I'll attest that hide-and-seek is no fun when played with a hysterical 8-year-old. I'm just thankful that I didn't have to post signs around the neighborhood: Lost Puppy – Last seen wearing a magenta one-piece bathing suit.

Sadie, now four months old, is fast. I, on the other hand, have a severely torn medial meniscus in my right knee, and in all likelihood, a small tear in my left one. I'm not fast. I'll never be able to run away from bullets.

Yesterday was rainy. I had an umbrella in one hand and a bag of poop and leash in the other. As I adjusted my hood, Sadie pulled the leash out of my hand and took off. We've been taking Sadie to obedience classes, but my desperate calls of "Come" were met with, "Come on, Daddy, try to catch me!" Sadie ran toward home and I ran after her. At least Mattie won't have to shoot me because I'll have a heart attack instead. Mattie could buy lots of dogs with the life insurance proceeds. I'd better not give her any ideas, or she'll be teaching Sadie the command "Run."

Sadie was almost home. I was in hot pursuit about 10 yards behind her when I saw a car coming toward us. My knees hurt. My heart pounded faster than on my honeymoon night.

"Please, please Sadie, turn right into the grass." Sadie turned left, directly into the path of the oncoming vehicle.

"Sadie, come! I won't let Jessie dress you in baby clothes anymore." I was way past panic mode. What if the driver was on the cell phone or worse yet, texting? I did what any brave man would do. I, too, turned left into the oncoming car's path and continued running toward it. I jumped up and down. If the meniscus in my left knee was slightly torn before, it's a large tear now. I waved my hands and umbrella in the air as if I'd just received my first six-figure advance check.

The car stopped. If it hadn't, I would have let it run over me. I'd rather go out as a courageous man trying to save his wife's puppy than by a bullet for losing it. Sadie covered the last few yards, ran up our driveway, and onto the porch. I reached the end of our driveway about 10 seconds later. I bent over, propped my hands on my aching knees, and tried to catch my breath. I wasn't tall. My hair was grayer and soaked with rain and sweat. I surely wasn't handsome. But at least I didn't have to walk into the house and tell Mattie, "Dog gone."

Wife or Dog

"You may kiss the bride." At 6'5", I leaned down and wrapped my arms around my 5'3" bride. I lifted her up, her feet completely off the ground, as we shared our first kiss as husband and wife. It didn't matter that giggles came from the congregation or that the pastor made a joke when Mattie's feet returned to the floor. I had just married my best friend. I sealed it with a kiss that we would remember. Over 27 years later, I'm still kissing the same woman.

So, when the time came to write an essay about my best friend, one would logically think I'd write about Mattie. As sports broadcaster, Lee Corso, says, "Not so fast, my friend!" You see, I'm an analyzer. I analyze everything from major purchases like a house or car, to minor purchases that involve grocery store coupons. Some, including me, might think I overanalyze.

I must say that Mattie is the leading candidate to be my best friend, but I'm going to take a few minutes to review. I've had some wonderful friendships through the years. And I can't forget man's best friend – my dog, Ginger. The analytical buttons in my head are turning fast. I think I'll go with Mattie ... no Ginger. On second thought, Mattie. Oh, but Ginger was such a devoted pet. I need to assess this a bit further.

Okay, Mattie did bear me a beautiful daughter. Point, Mattie. Come to think of it, I'll give her two points as a daughter is quite significant. Heck, breastfeeding alone deserved a few extra points, and I wouldn't want an epidural stuck in my back.

Ah, but Ginger excelled in obedience classes. When I'd say, "Come," she'd be by my side. Point, Ginger.

If I'd want to take a nap, Ginger would rest by my chair. Point, Ginger.

Mattie is my number one editor for my writing. A definite point for Mattie. However, sometimes her comments are less than diplomatic. Point deduction, Mattie.

When I'd read my work out loud to Ginger, she'd never call my column "boring." Point. Ginger. On the other hand, a good editor must provide constructive feedback. Point deduction, Ginger. Boy, this is going to be more difficult than I thought.

Mattie and I have been through so much over the years. She pushed me out of my comfort zone on numerous occasions. Mattie, 10-point deduction as I hated to get pushed. However, *because* of getting pushed I earned two college diplomas, a CPA license, and had a successful professional career. Mattie, 20 points. Mattie and I cried and held each other during the loss of loved ones. How can you place a point value on that? We shared in each other's successes and failures and made each other better people. Best friends are there for each other, right?

Of course, Mattie and I don't always see eye to eye. If it was only as simple as "come, sit, and stay." Two more points for Ginger. Then again, Mattie never needs to be let out in a rainstorm in the early morning hours to potty. Point deduction, Ginger. And I could do without picking up poop. Another point deduction, Ginger.

Conversely, I have to pick up after Mattie all the time. Mattie, five-point deduction for sloppiness.

I could go on and on, but I have a word limit. Unfortunately, Ginger's life had a limit, too. Her kidneys began to fail near the end of 2011. Mattie and I changed her diet. We sought the opinion of three vets. We spent years of royalty checks, not yet earned, on trips to the vet, tests, and medicine. I even learned to give Ginger fluids intravenously, a big deal for a man who hates to see blood and needles.

Though our hearts were breaking because Mattie and I knew the end was drawing near, we were more worried about how our then-7-year-old daughter would handle the loss of her "sister." Early one morning, Ginger suffered a stroke. It was easily my worst day as a father. I will never forget Jessie's wail. Mattie and I found ourselves in each other's arms again, with a little girl in between.

I dug a grave in the backyard and laid Ginger to rest. I placed a "Love" sign on top of her grave. Not a single day passes when I don't look out the house window to see "Love," and I remember Ginger, my best friend.

The List

One recent Saturday, Mattie attended a one-day conference. This allowed me to spend an entire day with Jessie. I informed Jessie I had a lot planned for our day.

She responded, "I'll make a list," and began immediately.

Minutes later, she presented me with a thorough, 18-item, typed list. As I glanced down the list, I noticed no afternoon nap scheduled for Daddy. I needed one by the time I finished reading the agenda, even though I had only been up for an hour.

Since I'm the boss, at least when Mattie's gone, I made a few tweaks to the schedule and printed a new copy. We had our game plan for the day. A few of the items were easy to check off the list.

"Get the mail." Jessie enjoys going to the mailbox to see what surprises await. When you're young, you don't pay attention to the bills.

"Eat lunch." Yay, Chick-fil-A.

A couple of the items were more time intensive. "Read while Daddy mows." Jessie sat on the front porch to read, while I finished mowing the front lawn before the forecasted rain arrived. "Go to Hobby Lobby." Jessie loves to go down *all* the aisles. Then there was item number 16, "Play with Daddy."

I smiled when I saw playtime with Dad made the list, but prior to playing, Jessie and I tackled the chores. We did well, too, completing 15 out of 18 items. Hobby Lobby took a lot out of me, even though we skipped a few aisles. I decided to exercise my right as boss to head home instead of going to Belk (item #8) and Walmart (item #11).

Now, all that remained on our list was "Play with Daddy." I offered to take Jessie to the baseball game. I even told her I'd buy her a soft pretzel. No, she had other games in mind. First, we played Old Maid. Ursula, the sea witch, was the old maid, as Jessie's deck had a Disney theme. Big smiles lit up our faces each time we pulled Ursula from the other's hand. I ended up being the old maid in game one. I thought about asking if that qualified me to take a nap, but I knew what Jessie's answer would be, so I saved my energy. In game two, I wasn't the old maid, though I didn't feel any younger.

Jessie then went to her closet for the next game, as "Play with Daddy" time had just begun. I thought she might pull out her chessboard. Instead, she brought her flowery shoulder bag containing two Barbie dolls with Barbie's combs, brushes, boots, shoes, blouses, and pants, plus Barbie's horse, and hair accessories for the dolls and the horse.

At this point, the baseball game was looking pretty good to me. "Jessie, I'll buy you cotton candy at the game, too." Shaking her head, she handed me a naked Barbie. I thought about exercising my "boss veto," but I could tell nude Barbie needed my help. So I found a nice halter top and covered her chest. Jessie helped me find a matching skirt. She told me Barbies don't wear panties. I then tried to get Barbie's boots on her, which took great effort. I brushed her hair and gave her a ponytail. I even found a pink hair accessory. Jessie asked for my help because she couldn't get her doll's pants up over her hips. Barbie must have put on a few pounds, but I finally got her dressed. In the meantime, Jessie pointed out that the halter top on my Barbie had come loose. I retied it to keep *all* of Barbie in. I brushed the horse's mane and tail, too. Jessie presented my jockey Barbie a trophy near the end of our playtime. Since I was the individual responsible for Barbie being clothed and on her well-groomed horse, I accepted the award.

Prior to bedtime, Jessie recorded her day's highlight in her daily journal. She wrote, "I had fun playing Barbie with Dad." And to think it could have boringly read, "I enjoyed eating a soft pretzel and cotton candy at the baseball game."

Each day, I wake up to a list that has more tasks than I could possibly complete in 24 hours. I must prioritize, and have faith that if I keep working hard, good things will happen. So I give each day my all, and, hopefully, by day's end, the list is shorter and I made an impact along the way.

Through the years, I've won a number of tennis trophies, which I proudly display on my bookshelf. They make me smile as I recall the fond times with my doubles partners and the blood and sweat we put forth to earn them. The jockey Barbie trophy measures only 1½ inches tall. It required no loss of blood or perspiration. But it is now one of my favorite trophies, because Jessie put "Play with Daddy" on her list and, in the eyes of my daughter, I came in first place.

Celebrate

5:30 a.m., Sunday, February 15, 1998. I hate it when the phone rings early in the morning, and not just because it wakes me up. My niece called to inform me that my older brother Phil had succumbed to cancer. I'll never forget Mattie's hug as we sobbed uncontrollably in each other's arms. It just couldn't be. He was only 46. My heart ached extra because I didn't get a chance to say goodbye, to give him one final hug and thank him for the impact he made on my life.

Just a few years earlier, it was Phil who woke me at 5:30 in the morning. It was my birthday. He said he was calling to help me get an early start so I could "celebrate all day long." I groggily thanked him, or at least I think I did. I know for sure I thanked him that night at 11:58 p.m. when I called to let him know that I was still celebrating.

Phil's life revolved around academia. After spending many years as a teacher, he moved into administration. One day, I came across his wooden paddle. Back in those days, paddling was still an acceptable form of punishment. I inquired jokingly how hard his spankings were, so he convinced me to bend over and grab my ankles. I'm almost positive that he swung with a little extra "oomph." What a great life lesson I learned that day. Think before you speak ... and especially before you bend over.

As my older brother, Phil took on a father-like role to me. While my dad, a self-employed mechanic, worked long hours in his garage to make ends meet, Phil stuck a baseball, football, basketball, and tennis racquet in my hand. Not only did he teach me the fundamentals of each sport, he challenged me to be the best I could be.

One of my best childhood memories was Phil hitting grounders to me at the ball diamond. I remember one game when I made four throwing errors to first base from my shortstop position. After the game, Phil hit grounder after grounder to me as I practiced my throws to first base. He taught me many life lessons through sports. We all make errors. The secret is to not give up and to keep working hard to get better.

Phil also introduced me to tennis. After each defeat, he would tease me with a Vince Lombardi quote or some other derisive comment to motivate me. I made it my mission to "take him down" no matter how long it took. When I won my first set against him after three years of failed attempts, I was so happy that I jumped not only the net on the court where we were playing, but all four nets inside the fence. Victory never tasted so sweet.

The tennis match I remember the most, though, was the only one we didn't complete. The heat index was near 120 degrees. What started out as play turned into misery, but it's hard to stop two stubborn competitors. We drenched the court with sweat. It became hard to breathe. We started to talk about the risks of heat stroke.

Finally, we came to our senses and agreed that a draw would be better than risking death or permanent disability from our stupidity. We ended up going down to his school so he could show me the new gymnasium. The wrestling mats were out on the floor. Before I knew it, he knocked me over, and I found myself in a wrestling match. He pinned me easily because he caught me completely off guard and I couldn't stop laughing long enough to make the match competitive. It wasn't what I had expected from an exhausted man in his 40s.

Many of Phil's students and colleagues will remember him for his numerous contributions to his school district. But, Phil was my teacher, too. As he stepped up to the plate or onto the courts, he taught me to always give it my best, no matter what the challenge.

Life brings victories and laughter, but also defeat and tears. The biggest lesson I learned from my brother's life, and death, is to cherish every moment and celebrate all day long.

Chapter 9

Conclusion

I've had lots of memorable MoMENts, sometimes as the teacher, and many times the willing or unwilling student. My parenting record is not perfect, but I've come a long way from that first diaper change. I can't believe how quickly time has sped by.

For the past 10-plus years, this stay-at-home dad has been blessed to watch Jessie grow. As Jessie begins her tween years, changes are becoming more frequent and drastic. A month ago, she wore a pair of her mom's shoes to church. Jessie's use of makeup, including mascara, has increased. A few weeks ago, I raised her bicycle seat and the whole seat pulled out of its holder. Since I couldn't raise it any higher, and Jessie's long legs couldn't pedal it like it was, we bought her a new bike. It's as tall as Mattie's.

How could Jessie have outgrown her bicycle? I just took off her training wheels, didn't I? Only yesterday, I guided her down the driveway, holding on tight so she wouldn't fall. Before I knew it, we were riding side by side through our neighborhood. Then suddenly, I'm holding her bike seat in my hand wondering why they don't make bikes that keep up with growing girls, and why girls grow too fast for their dads to keep up.

I guess, really, I'm pondering what happened and what's next? Apparently, fewer wagon rides. And more horse rides. Jessie took her first horseback-riding lesson this week and I'm afraid she's hooked. In fact, she left a few minutes ago with Mattie for another lesson. The last words I said to Jessie as she headed out the door were, "Hold on." I think, though, it's Dad who needs to "hold on" for the rides ahead, and I'm not just referring to horseback rides. But, whether I'm holding a bicycle seat, a saddle, or just holding on, I plan to celebrate life and remind readers to do the same.

I created the mnemonic "CHERISH" from the themes of chapters two through eight. If you're a new parent, about to become one, or have lots of experience, I hope you'll cherish the moments in your role as parent. Here's a snapshot of what I've learned during my tenure as a stay-at-home dad:

Class in Session – Be both a teacher and a student.

Hold On – To precious moments and sound mental health.

Energy – Lots is required.

Relax – Easier said than done, but try, both individually and as a couple.

I am Dad – I might not be "Superdad," but I can always be a loving dad.

Save me, Mom! – No one can take Mom's place.

Hodgepodge – Be prepared for anything and everything.

As a 55-year-old dad to a 10-year-old daughter, I hope I'll be present for all of Jessie's celebrations – high school and college graduations, marriage (if she finds her soulmate), and the birth of her children (if she chooses to have a family). I can't wait to see the mark she will make in the world; given her many talents and tenacity, I'm sure it will be a big one. I plan to add a few daddy-daughter doubles tennis trophies to my bookshelf, too.

I also realize more changes are on the horizon – additional sighs and surprises. In addition to the physical differences, like longer legs and bigger feet, I started to see personality changes when Jessie hit second grade. Before that she happily sat beside me at a football or basketball game. Then, she began to run off with her friends. Of course, I kept her in my view, and enjoyed seeing her have fun with the other kids, even as I missed having her with me. I won't forget the day I walked Jessie to her classroom and instead of a "Goodbye Daddy, I love you," she gave me a backward hand wave and rushed into her classroom to begin her day. I'm glad Jessie likes school, but a backward hand wave is a lousy substitute for a goodbye kiss.

Now that Jessie's a fourth grader, I no longer walk her to her classroom. Instead, I drop her off in front of the school and she rushes in to begin her day. This routine is better, in Jessie's opinion, because I have less chance of saying something that will embarrass her in front of her friends, like the morning I reminded her that "8 x 4 = 32" prior to a math test. Teachers, who probably get tired of parents hanging around the classroom distracting the kids, also seem to prefer the drop off and go approach. For me, however, it's just another step in the letting go process, even though I'd rather hold on … to more than a sweater, a sparkly purse, or a saddle.

As we giddy up into the future, Mattie and I will make it through the changes that lie ahead in Jessie's tween years, then hunker down for the teenage ones. We know that as she continues to mature into a beautiful, young lady, we'll be less involved in her life. She will be supported by her faith, her family and loved ones (including her dog), and a good attitude as she rides the roller coaster of life.

Last spring, I cleaned out my garage, a challenging project as there was more stuff than space. I found a spot to park Jessie's Radio Flyer wagon, even though it doesn't get used as frequently as in years past. Who knows, I might hang my long legs out, lift my feet, and let Jessie pull me. But, whether I'm the passenger or the chauffeur, I'll do my best, not simply to hold on, but to cherish the moments and celebrate all day long.

Epilogue

"Remember to cherish the moments." It's a fact that fathers and mothers face joys and challenges in raising their children. Yet, the 18 years we have our children at home zoom by.

Today, I joined my 10-year-old daughter and her 4-year-old cousin on the beach. They had a marvelous time building castles in the sand and running back and forth from the ocean with buckets of water to pour on their masterpiece. As I watched the two run, I wondered how Jessie went from 4 to 10. Like the tide sneaking in, you know it's going to happen and you can't stop it, but you don't always pay attention because it happens so gradually. I needed this reminder as I, like many others, struggle to find the right balance for the different demands on my time.

I hope this book has entertained and inspired you. That's my goal when I write, so it seems appropriate to close my first book with a wonderful email from Sara Stephens, Managing Editor of *Houston Family*. She thanked me "for writing so compellingly about cherishing the moments." My wish is that her touching email, excerpt copied below, will inspire you, too.

"You should also know that your writing has inspired me as a mother. For example, the other day my 6-year-old daughter stayed home from school. She felt okay, but had a low-grade fever the night before, and school rules dictate she had to stay home until she was 24 hours fever-free.

I was on deadline for the January issue and had a feature article due, which I had barely begun writing. Mostly, my daughter was quietly watching TV, with a few interruptions, but I kept my eye on the clock and felt good about meeting the deadline. Then my husband texted, inviting us to have lunch with him. I sighed. His work is a 20-minute-drive away. Then there's 45 minutes for eating and 20-minute drive back home. This would seriously impact my productivity. But, my husband rarely has time to meet for lunch, and I knew my daughter would enjoy the novelty of meeting him for lunch in town, so off we went. After lunch, my husband went back to work. As my daughter and I were headed out to the parking lot, she spotted an escalator (as you know, that's like a free rollercoaster for kids of certain age, and my daughter is just that age). It was monstrously high, and my daughter squealed with delight and begged me to go up. My schedule was already thrown off, and I thought, 'What difference could 5 minutes make?'

We went up, up, up the escalator, then down, down down. With a 'there, that wasn't so bad' lilt in my voice I said, 'Ok, that was fun, wasn't it? Let's get to the car now!' You can guess the response, 'Can we go up again? Just one more time? Pleeeease?' Reflexively, my throat tightened, ready to launch into a tense Mom-commando order, 'We went up once and now it's time to go.' But as my eyes met with hers, full of hope, excitement and sheer joy, a string of words flashed briefly, but brightly, in my brain: 'Cherish the moments.' I grabbed my daughter's hand, counted '1, 2, 3!' and jumped onto the escalator with her. On the ride up, we talked about how the escalator works (I think I made up something about hydraulics). When we got to the top, she turned to go back down, but I tugged gently on her arm and pointed to the end of the hallway above. 'Let's explore!' I urged. And off we went, stopping to look out the windows to see who could spot our car first, running up and down ramps, devising silly schemes for getting to the roof so we could 'rule the mall.' When we reached the other end of the corridor, we discovered another set of escalators.

'Shall we?' I said. And off we went: down, down, down, and up, up, up ….

By the time we got home from our adventure, the afternoon was shot. It was time to pick up my other daughter from school and start with the daily evening duties of homework, making dinner, etc. My writing deadline would have to wait. I missed my deadline. But I made a memory."

Sometimes you will never know the value of a moment until it becomes a memory.

– Dr. Seuss

Note:

This book began with an elevator ride in chapter 1 and ends with an escalator ride, which is appropriate as parenting is filled with many ups and downs. If something in this book inspires you to cherish a special moment, and you'd like to share it, please contact me at www.patrickhempfing.com.

DISCARD